100,000 MILES...
200,000 MILES... OR MORE
PRACTICAL CAR CARE

629.287   Wesner, James.
W   100,000 miles ... 200,000 miles ... or more
         : practical car care / by James Wesner, with
         Joe Ettwein. -- Blue Ridge Summit, Pa. : TAB
         Books, 1988.

           180 p. : ill.   10708

           Includes index.
           ISBN 0-8306-9367-X(pbk.) : $10.95

                                        FEB 89

           1. Automobiles--Maintenance and repair.
         I. Ettwein, Joe. II. Title.

                                        14

                                   88-22741

This book is dedicated to:

Paul and Jonathan

and

Eric, Brad, Scott

and

Laura

100,000 MILES...
200,000 MILES... OR MORE
PRACTICAL CAR CARE

JAMES WESNER WITH JOE ETTWEIN

TAB BOOKS Inc.
Blue Ridge Summit, PA

FIRST EDITION
FIRST PRINTING

Library of Congress Cataloging in Publication Data

Wesner, James.
   100,000 miles— 200,000 miles— or more : practical car care / by
James Wesner, with Joe Ettwein.
      p.   cm.
   Includes index.
   ISBN 0-8306-9067-0   ISBN 0-8306-9367-X (pbk.)
      1. Automobiles—Maintenance and repair. I. Ettwein, Joe.
II. Title.   III. Title: One hundred thousand miles— two hundred
thousand miles— or more.
TL152.W448 1988   88-22741
629.28′722—dc19   CIP

TAB BOOKS Inc. offers software for sale. For information and
a catalog, please contact TAB Software Department, Blue Ridge
Summit, PA 17294-0850.

Questions regarding the content of this book
should be addressed to:

   Reader Inquiry Branch
   TAB BOOKS Inc.
   Blue Ridge Summit, PA 17294-0214

Contents

Acknowledgments

Bethlehem Automatic Transmissions, Bethlehem, Pennsylvania
Champion Spark Plug Company, Toledo, Ohio
Master Mechanics, Inc., Bethlehem, Pennsylvania
The Goodyear Tire and Rubber Company, Akron, Ohio

Introduction

We sincerely hope you enjoy this book on car care. It's been a long time in the writing, and we feel that for the consumer, it is long overdue. We thank you for spending your money and your time on the book. We are certain you will benefit greatly from your purchase.

We wrote this book both from the engineer's and the mechanic's point of view. The engineer's point of view provides you with the design background you will need to make intelligent decisions regarding the care of your car. The mechanic's point of view provides you with practical advice on car care and tempers the engineer's input with years of daily, automotive servicing experience.

Please read and use this book with an open mind. Don't place much stock in all the well-meant, free advice you get from so-called "car buffs" or "experts" at work or in school. They might know a thing or two, but unless their cars are running in the 100,000 mile range they might not qualify as the best source of information.

This book will provide you with the theory and practical background you will need to get long life from your car, perhaps 100,000, or even 200,000 or more miles. The material presented here does not, with the exceptions in Chapter 16, provide instructions for performing the necessary car care. The material in this book does not explain how to do major maintenance and repair or what tools or accessory equipment you need to do the job. When changing your car oil filter for example, we explain why you would want to do it, the recommended frequency of changing the oil and filter and, perhaps, some related practical advice such as oil types or kinds of filters available.

Information on actually performing the less routine or more complicated car care is available from your car manufacturer in the form of shop manuals, or in any number of fine publications on the subject at your local bookstore.

Finally, remember that properly caring for your car can be a most rewarding experience. The feeling you will get knowing you have a smooth-running, ready-to-perform car at your disposal is easy to envision. The feeling you will get knowing your car dealer isn't dipping into your bank account every two to four years will be a welcome one if you are one of the many people who have to buy cars that often because of car care neglect.

Money Matters

"WELL, I DON'T KNOW. IS THAT THE BEST YOU CAN DO?" SAID TOM, A PROSPECTIVE CAR buyer.

"If you don't drive it on outta here someone else will. They're selling like hotcakes," said Delbert, Ace Motors salesman.

"We can't afford these ridiculous payments. I guess the new deck and the kitchen remodeling will have to wait," said Tom to his wife Joan.

"Listen, Delbert, my old car should be worth a lot more than you're offering me for it on the trade-in. How 'bout upping your offer," said Tom.

"Well, I'll have to check with the boss. Be right back," said Delbert as he left.

"Joan, we just have to get out from under these constant car payments. I wish we would have taken better care of our old car," said Tom.

"Sorry, Tom, Joan," said Delbert when he returned. "The boss says it'll take maybe $1500 to $2000 just to fix up your old car so we can sell it. Our final price stands," said Delbert.

"Tom, let's just sign and get this over with. We need the new car and I just don't see any other way to go right now," said Joan.

"I guess you're right, honey. We're stuck once again. Why don't they build cars to last any more?" asked Tom as he pleaded with Delbert.

"We just sell 'em and fix 'em Tom. We don't design 'em. Now Tom, sign right here. And Joan, you sign here," instructed Delbert.

Sound familiar? Unfortunately that's just what most people go through every 2 to 4 years, whether they buy a new or a used car. It doesn't have to be that way, however. We can, to a large degree, control our automotive destiny.

Did you ever notice the older couple driving around town in the 1953 DeSoto? Let's call them Mr. and Mrs. Miller. It's true that they don't drive much. However, next time you see them, follow them home (just pretending), and watch what Mr. Miller does after he parks the car in the garage.

He probably wipes down the car body with a soft rag, checks the oil, sniffs around for any strange odors and, generally gives "ole Bessy" the once over. If he notices anything out of the ordinary, he'll have Jakey down at the garage look into it. He and Jakey have been doing business for 30 odd years now. Mr. Miller keeps a maintenance checklist hanging by the garage door and checks it for any upcoming maintenance activities before he joins Mrs. Miller for a snack in the house. Jakey knows about Mr. Miller's maintenance checklist and together they confer on it often.

So what's Mr. Miller's secret? Let's pull it out of the story by the numbers.

1. He doesn't drive much.
2. He keeps his car in a garage.
3. He keeps the body clean.
4. He regularly checks the oil.
5. He gives his car the "once over" regularly.
6. He takes care of problems as soon as they arise.
7. He has a qualified mechanic whom he has known for many years do his maintenance and repair work.
8. He keeps a maintenance checklist and checks it often.
9. He keeps his mechanic apprised of his maintenance checklist and discusses it with him.
10. He's obviously proud of his car and has even given it the nickname "ole Bessy." After all, how could he let a family member like "ole Bessy" run down!

You can do what Mr. Miller does and avoid Delbert at Ace Motors. It's not difficult and it doesn't take a lot of time. Before we go any further, we would like to show you just how much money you can save by properly caring for your car. By the way, the next section serves as the most outstanding justification for following the advice in this book. You will save thousands of dollars and come out way ahead of all your neighbors and friends. While they are making their car payments, you will have money in the bank.

A YEARLY EVENT

Every year about mid-September it's the same fanfare: a parade of new cars from out of the manufacturers' doors or off the drive ramps at the dock. Millions are spent on advertising to appeal to your desires for that new car. There's a lot of psychology to it, and for the most part, it works very well.

So you buy your new car. It runs great, feels great, even smells great. We don't like to spoil your fun, but there is something you have to be aware of in regard to your new car that you might not be aware of now. It's called depreciation. It begins to eat away at the value of your car like a cancer as soon as you take possession. In fact, the day after you drive that new mechanical marvel home, it could have already lost up to $1,000 in value.

Where did that money go? Well, it's really in the salesman's pocket—and you put it there. This might seem almost criminal, but sorry, you can't press charges because it's all legal. It is not against the law for a fool to part with his money unless he is defrauded. Car dealers don't have to fraud anyone to remain in business. They're just happy to take your money. Let's talk money now.

ECONOMICS

It will help to understand a few accounting definitions before we get into the real meat of the subject:

- Present worth (P)—the present sum of money for which you promise to make specified future payments.
- Future worth (F)—the sum of money at the end of a number of payments from the present date; is equivalent to the present worth with interest.
- Interest (i)—an interest rate for a certain period of time, or money paid for the use of borrowed money.
- Compound interest—the interest each year based on the total amount owed at the end of the previous year. The total amount includes the original principal plus the accumulated interest that had not been paid when due.
- Principal—the original amount of a loan.
- Incremental payments (installments)—all such future payments or series of payments that will repay a given principal plus interest.
- Annual payment (A)—the end of period payment or receipt in a uniform series, continuing for the number of periods. The entire series is equivalent to P at interest rate.

The basic question we want to answer is: Given a certain time period, is it more economically sound to buy a new car, a used car, or keep up the old car?

Let's say our new car costs $12,000. The interest rate is 10% per year (or 10%/12 = 0.833% per month). The loan will be for 4 years, or 48 months. Also, let's further suppose we have a car to trade in (or sell privately) that will be worth $4,000. First we want to find out what our annual payment (A) is going to be on the loan. We'll use the definitions given previously.

$$P = \$12,000 - \$4,000 = \$8,000 \text{ (We are not financing the \$4,000)}$$
$$i = 10\% \ (0.1)$$
$$n = 4 \text{ years}$$
$$A = \text{Unknown}$$

To find A: $A = P[\,i(1 + i)^n\,] \div [(1 + i)^n - 1]$

Then $A = \$8,000\ [0.1(1 + 0.1)^4] \div [(1 + 0.1)^4 - 1] = \$2,523.76$ annual interest.

Then the total car payment for 4 years would be $4 \times A = 4 \times \$2,523.76 = \$10,095.04$

The original price minus the trade-in value was identified as P = $8,000. Therefore, the total of all interest payments is $10,095.04 − $8,000 = $2,095.04.

Next, we want to find the total paid-out cost for the new car for 4 years. We will not add gasoline, oil, or license costs, however. Some realistic numbers might be as follows:

$10,095 for loan payments (previously determined above)
$ 2,800 for insurance ($700 per year is modest)
$ 1,000 maintenance (an average over 4 years for a new car)
$13,895 total paid-out cost of new car

That's what you will pay for the new car. Now, when you consider you also traded your old car you should add the $4,000 value to the paid-out total. All told; you have $17,895 tied up in a four-year-old *used* car!!

By the way of comparison, let's see where you would be financially if you had kept the old car and had not bought the new car. First, we know we won't have any car payments. We will have insurance and maintenance as before, however. Again we won't add gasoline, oil or license costs.

$ 0 for loan payments
$1,600 for insurance ($400 per year for a used car is average)
$2,000 maintenance (an average over 4 years for a used car)
$3,600 total paid-out cost of old car

Again, add the $4,000 value of the car, and you have $7,600 tied up in the old car. That's a savings of $10,295 in 4 years ($17,895 − $7,600).

Note that the $4,000 value of the old car was not depreciated over the 4 years for ease of comparison. Actually, the value of the old car after 4 years may be about $1,000 or less. If you were going to use it as a trade-in for a newer car, at the end of 4 years you would have to properly account for it. You can do this by assigning a $1,000 trade-in value for the old car in the example and, say, a $5,000 trade-in value for the new car in the example at the end of 4 years. You will still be way ahead of the game by maintaining the old car.

Quite simply, you need to start taking care of your car. There are not too many people who can honestly afford to give up over $10,000 or more, as in our example, every 4 years for a new car. Look at the cold, hard facts when deciding on a change of cars. Don't let the car manufacturers sway your decision with their clever advertising. They're good at it, but, you can beat them.

Read the rest of this book and learn how you can keep that car of yours looking and running great.

The Philosophy of Car Care

WHY DEFINE PHILOSOPHY IN A BOOK ABOUT CAR CARE AND MAINTENANCE? BECAUSE WE want to introduce an entirely different way of thinking—a new philosophy about the way you take care of your car. It is important that you understand the material in this chapter if you are to successfully apply the theory and recommendations contained in the remainder of this book.

In our philosophy of car care, we attempt to provide guidance and to resolve questions on car care so that your car can have a long and relatively trouble-free life. In effect, we are striving to formulate the standards against which you may judge your own actions in regard to caring for your car.

THE PROUD JAPANESE

Detroit has learned a lot from the Japanese auto manufacturers, who in the not-too-distant past learned a lot from Detroit. There was a time when American cars were just about the best assembly line automobile available in the world at a price the public could afford. The Japanese learned our secrets of pride of workmanship and quality in the early 1950s, and they have built upon it ever since.

Detroit, however, got sidetracked and began to neglect quality. Why did it happen? Because Detroit felt the Japanese and European auto makers would never offer any serious competition. Also, after World War II the only thing that seemed to matter to big businesses was the bottom line on the accounting sheets. No matter that the cars Detroit made were not the quality product they used to be, just so long as they sold and the money kept coming in. Fortunately, that attitude has recently been changing for the better. But back to the Japanese.

The Japanese people are proud of what they have accomplished and of what they own. They are an island nation with a large population, little land area, and nowhere to expand. Most things need to be imported—such as fuel, raw materials, and food. The Japanese cannot afford to waste what they have; they don't live in a throw-away society as we do. They have to keep their cars in good condition because it simply costs too much to do otherwise. There's more to their story, however.

Public pride and community standing are extremely important to the Japanese. Their culture is such that to be shamed in public is a terrible thing. The car owned by a Japanese family is an important extension of that cultural pride. To be seen in public with a dirty car or one that smokes because of burning oil would be shameful, indeed. In Japan you see very few dirty cars on the roads, mechanical repairs are taken care of quickly by the owners. The ''old bomb'' trailing a smoke screen, a common sight in the United States, is seldom seen in Japan.

In sum, the Japanese retain pride of ownership, pride in themselves, and pride in manufacturing a quality product—admirable qualities. Have we lost these in ourselves? We think not. Perhaps, like a Sunday afternoon pass receiver in the football game with jittery hands, we've just fumbled the ball a little, but retained possession.

TAKING CARE OF WHAT YOU OWN

The philosophy and economic principles outlined here will apply to any purchase or situation. They apply whether you own a refrigerator, air conditioner, motorcycle, or house. The better care you take of what you own and the longer you keep it, the better off you will be financially. Remember: the more you own, the more you have to maintain and fix. So live the simple life. Don't buy three cars when one or two will do.

Car care is simple. You don't have to be a college graduate with an engineering degree or a licensed mechanic with 25 years experience to properly maintain your car. This book, beginning with Chapter 3, tells you what has to be done, why it has to be done, and when or how often a particular maintenance activity needs to be performed to obtain long car life. If you're going to tackle your own maintenance we suggest you buy a good how-to book on the subject. However, stick with the intervals of maintenance recommended here. Also, there are many fine auto repair courses available through community colleges, high school evening programs, vocational-technical schools, and correspondence courses. Chapter 16 then provides some basic instructions on performing some of the easier, routine maintenance we discuss throughout the book.

It's not so important who does the work as that the required work gets done properly and at the required time or interval. If you want to do the work yourself and you have the time and tools, by all means go ahead and do it. There are advantages and disadvantages you will want to consider.

You will get satisfaction and save big money by doing the work yourself. Knowing you can handle most maintenance jobs without a mechanic will give you a sense of pride and independence. You will be the only one, for the most part, who touches your car and you will know its idiosyncrasies better than anyone. There are some jobs you might not want to handle, like transmission maintenance, but they are few in number. The only disadvantages in doing your own work are the time you will have to invest and the additional financial burden of providing yourself with some extra tools. Of course, you can always perform the simple maintenance items yourself, leaving the more difficult or time-consuming ones, or those that require special tools, to your mechanic.

There are advantages in having your car care work done by your mechanic. First of all, the time you save might be more valuable to you than the money saved by doing your own work. That's a personal decision you will have to make. Plus, if you're not comfortable with tools or you don't feel sufficiently qualified, perhaps allowing your mechanic to repair or maintain your car is the best option.

Finding a Good Mechanic

In a recent study done by the Department of Transportation, 53% of the money for auto repairs was spent on unnecessary or improper repairs. Brock Adams, Transportation Secretary at the time of the report, said: "When we took test cars into repair shops at random, we found we had only a 50-50 chance of getting a car fixed right, and for the right price. We found it was almost a sure thing that the shop would do something wrong on the engine."

You can see why choosing a good and honest mechanic is important. And by performing the recommended service outlined in this book, your chances of keeping your car out of the shop in the first place are much improved. It is the best way to avoid incompetent auto repair and even fraud.

When choosing a mechanic, the recommendations provided by friends are a good bet. Most people won't stick with an incompetent mechanic or one they feel they can't trust. Also, check on the mechanic's reputation with the Better Business Bureau. They can tell you about any customer complaints registered with them. In addition, check for mechanic certification by the National Institute for Automotive Service Excellence (NIASE).

The NIASE conducts programs of testing for auto mechanics on various automotive systems. A mechanic can be certified in one or all of the subject areas. Certified mechanics wear a patch on their sleeve testifying to their areas of expertise. Recertification is necessary every 5 years.

The shop should be neat and uncluttered but not necessarily spotless. There should not be tools scattered all over the place. Parts should be next to the cars they belong with. You can't expect a good shop to sparkle like your bathroom, but you should expect a shop to be efficient and well organized.

What about personal qualities? Is the mechanic willing to spend time with you? Does he give you flippant answers to your questions? Is he courteous? Does he make you feel as if you don't know anything about cars? Does he leave you with a "take it or leave it" attitude? Ask yourself these questions when deciding on a mechanic.

A good idea is to get to know a prospective mechanic slowly. Start by buying some replacement bulbs or a fan belt from him. Get to know him on a first-name basis. Then give him a small job to do like changing your oil or spark plugs. Judge his work and his price and go from there. Construct a mutual trust and you will never regret it.

For some jobs like front-end alignment, and for tire, muffler, and shock absorber replacements, check out the many specialty shops that do this kind of work. Their work will be faster and their guarantees might be good for the life of the car. Chances are their prices will be lower, too.

Tools

The following is a list of tools you will need if you decide to do your own car maintenance.

1. Shop manuals—available through new car auto dealers
2. Socket set—6mm to 19mm or ⅜ inch to ¾ inch
3. Open-end wrench set—6mm to 19mm or ⅜ inch to 1 inch
4. Box-end wrench set—6mm to 19mm or ⅜ inch to 1 inch
5. Allen wrench set—2mm to 10mm or .050 inch to .250 inch
6. Flex-head ⅜-inch drive ratchet
7. 3-inch and 6-inch drive extensions—⅜-inch drive
8. U-joint connector—⅜-inch drive
9. 0- to 150-pound torque wrench—⅜-inch drive
10. Adjustable wrenches—½-inch and 1½-inch jaws
11. Flat blade screwdrivers—⅛ inch, ¼ inch, ⅜ inch, and stubby
12. Philips screwdrivers—Numbers 1, 2, 3, 4, and stubby
13. Slip-joint pliers
14. Needle-nose pliers
15. Wire cutter/stripper
16. Set of tubing wrenches
17. Distributor wrench
18. Oil-filter wrench
19. Nut driver set—metric or U.S.
20. Spark plug wrench
21. Feeler gauges—metric or U.S.
22. Tire pressure gauge—0 to 60 psi
23. Tire tread depth gauge
24. Belt tension gauge
25. 16-ounce ball-peen hammer
26. Soldering gun
27. Timing light
28. Tach/dwell meter
29. Compression tester
30. Continuity tester
31. Distributor-points file—not applicable for electronic ignitions, but can be used as a spark plug file
32. Grease gun
33. Battery hydrometer
34. Scissors jack—2-ton capacity
35. Four jack stands—1½-ton capacity each
36. Oil drain pan
37. Oil can spout
38. Inspection mirrors
39. Pocketknife
40. Toolbox
41. Chamois
42. Rags

Don't buy cheap tools, they just don't last and might even cause damage or injury when used. If you can amass the above tool collection, you will be able to perform any maintenance activity described in this book, except where noted. You can plan on spending up to $500 on these tools. They will pay for themselves in perhaps as little as a year or two.

3

Oil Lubrication

THIS CHAPTER AND THE NEXT ARE THE TWO MOST IMPORTANT CHAPTERS IN THIS BOOK, with regard to the mechanical care of your car. Read them carefully, because if you grasp the theory and follow the recommendations, your car engine will stand an excellent chance of performing reliably without the need for repair for many years.

THEORY OF LUBRICATION

Engine friction caused by the sliding of pistons against cylinder walls, the rotation of journals in bearings, and the relative movement of many different engine parts one to another is responsible for producing wear and generating some of the heat in your car engine. Friction caused by metal contact between the various surfaces in your car engine can be drastically reduced by the presence of a lubricant, commonly engine oil.

The lubricant does its job remarkably well, so long as it is kept clean and doesn't get too hot. Engine lubricants actually function to separate two surfaces in relative motion and so reduce metal contact. They perform this task by filling minute depressions in metal that are caused by the machining process used to manufacture the parts. In addition, the lubricant "plates" all the ridges caused by machining with a thin layer of oil molecules, or in some oils, an oil additive (Fig. 3-1).

There are many different parts in your car that require lubrication. The crankshaft, for example, is one of the more important of these. The part of the crankshaft (or any other shaft, such as a camshaft) that rides in a bearing is called a journal (Fig. 3-2). When the shaft is not moving (engine off), its weight allows the journal to contact the bearing

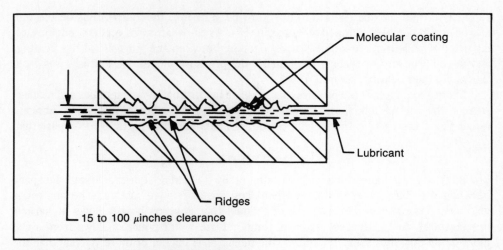

Fig. 3-1. Oil molecules coating metallic surfaces.

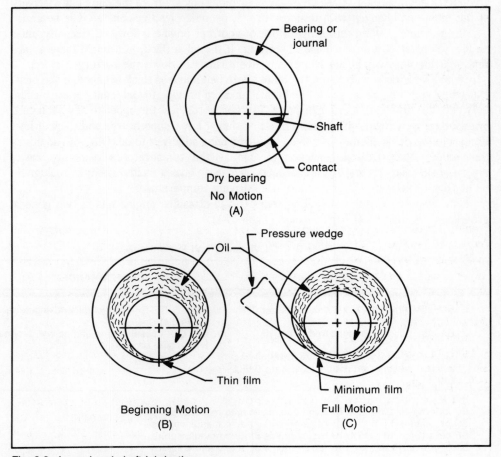

Fig. 3-2. Journal and shaft lubrication.

as in (A). When the shaft starts to turn (engine start up), the journal rolls on the thin film or coating of oil mentioned above as in (B)). As the shaft turns further (engine running), oil is pulled into a wedge-shaped opening between the journal and the bearing, and the oil pressure increases. Eventually, the pressure moves the journal away from the wall of the bearing, as in (C).

Lubrication, then, is the process that modifies the frictional characteristics and reduces wear at the surface interface between two or more parts when in motion. A lubricant (engine oil in this case) is the medium introduced between such parts to accomplish this.

VISCOSITY

You might ask what keeps the oil from being easily washed or squeezed out of the space between the surfaces of the parts when they are in relative motion. The answer is viscosity. Viscosity is the property of a liquid that governs how it flows at various temperatures and pressures. At room temperature, water pours or flows from a cup more easily than molasses. Therefore, the molasses is thicker or more viscous than the water. The viscosity of most liquids is dependent upon temperature. In our example, if you heat the molasses, it will gradually pour more quickly from the cup. The viscosity of the molasses changes with temperature; it becomes less viscous as it is heated.

In the winter, when the temperature of your car engine is low, oil viscosity must be low (oil must be thin) for ease of starting. If the oil is thick, you might have a hard time starting your car in the winter and eventually run down the battery.

When the engine warms up, the oil tends to become less thick because of the heat. But when your engine is hot, it needs thicker oil to provide for adequate lubricant film between the surfaces of its running parts. In other words, just the opposite of what nature intended for most fluids. Engine oils must be thin at low temperatures and thick at high temperatures. This dilemma is solved by introducing additives to oil. Oils with additives that modify their natural tendency to thin as the temperatures rises are called multiviscosity oils. Our first recommendation is to use a quality multiviscosity or multigrade oil in your car engine for protection at all driving temperatures.

The Society of Automotive Engineers (SAE) classifies engine oils in two general groupings: viscosity and performance (Table 3-1).

Table 3-1. Oil Viscosity and Performance.

VISCOSITY	PERFORMANCE
1. SAE 5W, 10W, 20W, 25W measured at 0°F	1. SC, SD, SE, SF—oils for general engine service (see note)
2. SAE 20, 30, 40, 50 measured at 210°F	2. CC, CD—diesel engine and heavy, dirty gasoline engine service
3. Multigrade—those that have viscosity characteristics meeting requirements at both 0°F & 210°F	
NOTE: SC oil—meets 1964 to 1967 requirements of auto manufacturers SD oil—meets 1968 to 1971 requirements of auto manufacturers SE oil—meets 1972 to 1979 requirements of auto manufacturers SF oil—meets 1980 to 1986 requirements of auto manufacturers	

Always use an oil with the minimum rating for performance as specified for your car year. You may upgrade. For example, you can use SF grade oil for any of the model years shown. SF grades, by the way, were specially formulated for emission-controlled engines.

Correct oil viscosity is important to engine performance. If the viscosity is too high, the engine will need to work harder to pump the oil and move it around to the different engine parts to be lubricated. This results in reduced engine power, and fuel consumption is increased as much as 15 percent. If the viscosity is too low, sealing between the piston rings and cylinder will be poor. The increased blowing of oil past the rings and into the combustion chamber therefore increases oil consumption. To get the best all-around performance use a 10-W30 or 10-W40 oil.

Although a 10-W30 oil satisfies precisely only the 10W and 30 specifications, it can also serve as a 20 oil, since in operating between 10W to 30 it passes the 20 characteristic line. The same is true of the 10-W40 oil.

MORE ABOUT OIL

Lubricating oil is made up of a base oil and additives. Together these must reduce wear, remove heat caused by friction and fuel burning, and prevent accumulation of deposits in the engine. The base oil is usually a mineral oil, sometimes it is synthetic. Additives provide additional performance characteristics that the mineral oil alone does not have. Let's discuss base oils first.

Mineral or petroleum oils are used as the base oil in engine lubricating oils because of their moderate cost and suitability with the many materials that make up the engine parts. They are refined from various crude oils of which there are three main types: Paraffin-based or Pennsylvania crude, naphthene-based or Texas crude, and those that are a mix of both. Years ago a paraffin-based oil would have been the best choice for use in your engine, because the naphthene-based oils contained a lot of asphalt which, if not removed, can damage your engine. Modern refining methods successfully remove asphalt to a degree that a naphthene-based oil is entirely satisfactory for use. We, therefore, do not recommend any specific oil; just stick with a national brand.

Synthetic lubricants are sometimes used as a base oil. These lubricants are man-made organic chemicals. They were originally developed by the aircraft industry to serve the high speed and operating temperatures of jet aircraft engines. Normally, they are used only in specialty applications such as instruments, hydraulic systems, and in heat transfer systems. Their disadvantage in auto engine use is their high cost. However, it is claimed that these lubricants stay cleaner longer and, therefore, engine oil changes are less frequent. You can use them if you like, but their benefits are still being tested, so it's probably best to stick with natural oils.

Base oils are only half the story on engine lubricating oils. During the refining process certain compounds are removed that are highly effective as lubrication. Also, the properties of mineral oil are not sufficiently strong to stand up to the conditions in a high-performance engine. For these reasons, mineral oils are doctored by the addition of chemicals that will allow the oil to do its job. The only additive we will discuss in detail is the detergent-dispersant additive. For a listing and brief explanation of the more common additives, see Table 3-2. All the better national brands of engine oil contain these and other additives.

Table 3-2. Engine Oil Additives.

Additive Type	Reason for Use	Effect
Detergent-Dispersant	Maintains engine cleanliness	Keeps oil-soluble material in suspension
Viscosity index improver*	Lowers the rate of change of viscosity with temperature	Stabilizes abrupt viscosity changes
Oxidation inhibitor	Retards oxidative decomposition of the oil	Reduces varnish, sludge, and corrosion
Corrosion inhibitor	Prevents attack of corrosive oil contaminants on bearing and other engine parts	Reduces wear, increases engine life
Metal deactivator	Passivates metal surfaces	Inhibits oxidation of engine parts
Anti-wear extreme pressure (EP), and oiliness film strength agents	Reduces friction	Prevents scoring and seizure. Reduces wear
Rust inhibitor	Prevents rusting of ferrous engine parts	Protects during storage and from acidic moisture during cold engine operation
Pour point depressant**	Lowers pour point of lubricant	Reduces effects of wax in the oil when starting a cold engine. Reduces wear at startup
Foam inhibitor	Prevents formation of foam	Prevents air entrainment in the oil, which results in adverse effects on oil pressure and heat transfer.

*A measure of the rate of change of viscosity with temperature. In general, oil having a high viscosity index (VI) has a better temperature-viscosity relationship than oil with a low VI; better meaning the rate of change of viscosity with temperature is less.
**The pour point of an oil is determined by lowering the temperature of the oil in a test jar until no movement of the oil (within 5 seconds) occurs when the test jar is moved from a vertical to a horizontal position. The pour point of an oil is important only for low engine temperature operation.

It is important to know about detergent-dispersant additives because engine oils are available as both detergent and non-detergent types. Thus, as a consumer you have a choice to make. Let's discuss exactly how this type of additive works.

As far as is known, the detergent-dispersant additives commonly used in engine oils chemically unite with the compounds in the oil that tend to form sludge and varnish. This chemical action prevents deposits and removes built-up deposits. Also, by this chemical action, the deposits are neutralized and do not cling to surfaces. The deposits are kept dispersed or suspended in the oil and are eventually removed in part through action of the engine oil filter.

Varnish is a hard, lustrous, oil-insoluble deposit that forms on the piston. It must be removed by a solvent. It is formed by oxidation of hydrocarbons in oil exposed to high temperatures. The highest temperature the engine oil experiences is at the piston skirt, hence, the formation of varnish there. The same materials that form varnish can coagulate with carbon, oil, water, and dirt in the crankcase to form sludge. Sludge is a black mud that can be removed by wiping. The presence of water in the crankcase is the major cause of sludge formation.

Water collects in the crankcase in two ways. Because it is a product of fuel combustion, the hydrogen in the fuel combines with the oxygen in the air to form water. Most of this water is exhausted as a vapor with other hot gases in the exhaust. Some condensation does occur as the engine cools, and this condensed water can leak past the piston rings into the crankcase. Another way water finds its way to the crankcase, and hence the engine oil, is from the crankcase ventilating system. When the engine is cold, moisture in the air drawn through the crankcase by the ventilating system may condense on cold engine parts and leak into the crankcase. This problem has been significantly reduced with the newer closed crankcase ventilation systems and the recirculation of exhaust gases that quickly warm the engine.

The deposits formed by chemical action of the detergent-dispersant additive show up in the oil as black particles. Because these black particles are carried in the oil, the color of the oil will be dark brown or even black. A non-detergent oil would not exhibit this coloration. So, don't be alarmed by the dirty color of the detergent oil—this proves that the oil is doing its job. A non-detergent oil will not prevent sludge and varnish formation. The oil will look a beautiful golden yellow because the sludge and varnish are left in the engine where they cause wear and foul oil passages. Our recommendation is to always use detergent-type oil.

As the detergent-dispersant additive continues to chemically unite with sludge and varnish-forming compounds in the oil, it will eventually be used up. Once this occurs, the oil will rapidly become polluted. Tests have shown that once the detergent-dispersant additive is 50% consumed, the remaining detergent-dispersant additive is of insufficient concentration to remove sludge and varnish from the engine. In most cars the detergent-dispersant additive reaches the 50% strength level after approximately 2,000 to 3,000 miles of operation. This eventually occurs with any type of additive, so changing the oil is very important. Based on this, we recommend changing the oil every 3,000 miles or sooner. This might seem too frequent, but for the average driver, it is only three to four times a year. This is probably the most important recommendation in this book.

Be cautious in changing from a non-detergent to a detergent oil. If you have been using a non-detergent oil, your engine has probably accumulated large amounts of sludge. With the change to a detergent oil, the detergent additive loosens all of the deposits and very quickly overloads the oils ability to carry the deposits in suspension. The deposits will break away from engine surfaces and accumulate as a large mass at the pump strainer. When this happens, lubrication is interrupted and engine failure ensues. To avoid this, drain the detergent oil after only a few hours of operation—or sooner if coloration or appearance indicate fouling. Then refill with fresh oil, run 1,500 miles, change to fresh oil again, and follow our recommended oil change interval.

DIRT

Another reason to change engine oil frequently is to eliminate the formation of large quantities of dirt within the oil. Dirt can get into the engine in numerous ways. Inefficient or loose air filters allow passage of dirt through the carburetor and may be the single largest source of such violation. In addition, leaking gaskets, fouled fuel filters, loose oil filler caps, and use of filthy tools when servicing are all sources of dirt.

To illustrate how important it is to keep dirt particles out of the engine, let's take a look at bearing design and, in particular, bearing clearances (Fig. 3-3). Radial clearance (C) is equal to the bearing bore radius (R) minus the journal radius (r), as shown. Radial bearing clearance in new engines is of the order 0.0015 inches and smaller. That is a very small distance indeed. Any dirt particle 0.0015 or smaller that manages to wedge between the journal and bearing could scratch these surfaces, causing wear and decreased bearing and journal life. That is the reason engine oil must be kept as free of dirt as possible. Radial clearance increases with engine age, so it is more important to maintain

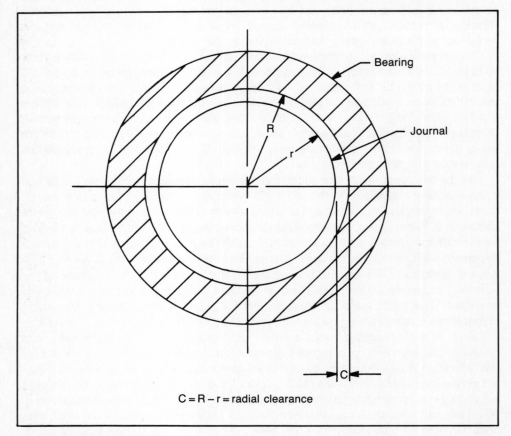

C = R – r = radial clearance

Fig. 3-3. Bearing clearance.

a schedule of frequent oil changes while the engine is young and clearances are tight. Along with frequent oil changes, another way to keep oil relatively dirt-free is to frequently change the oil filter.

OIL FILTERS

All automotive engines have oil filters that remove, for a time, particles of dirt less than 1 micron (0.000034 inches) in size from the engine oil. Eventually, all oil filters become clogged and must be removed and replaced. There are two main types of oil filters: by-pass and full flow.

In bypass filtering (Fig. 3-4) most of the oil flow (about 90%) goes from the oil pump to the engine bearings. A much smaller quantity (about 10%) will bypass the bearings and flow through the oil filter. With this method, the oil filter material can be made dense enough to filter dirt particles down to 1 micron in size. However, not all of the oil is adequately filtered because of the bypass.

With full-flow filtering (Fig. 3-5) 100% of the oil is pumped through the oil filter for very efficient filtering. The one drawback to full-flow filtering is that the filter medium must be less dense to allow full oil flow without excessive pump pressure. This

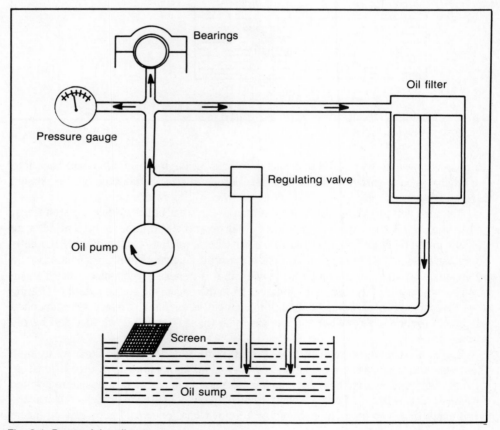

Fig. 3-4. Bypass lube oil system.

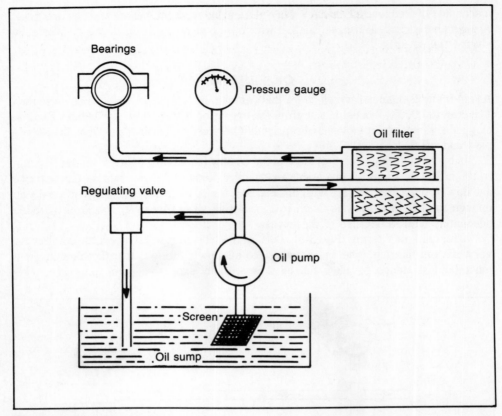

Fig. 3-5. Full flow lube oil system.

arrangement will allow small dirt particles to pass through the oil filter and back into the engine. These particles can be several microns in size. If this type of filter should become clogged, a relief valve will allow oil flow to bypass the filter.

Abrasive dirt particles in the engine oil can cause wear of the cylinder, piston rings, and bearings. That is why it is imperative that engine oil be kept clean. The filtering medium in the oil filter that removes these particles is made of cotton, paper, synthetic fibers, or cellulose. One might think that a constant change of filtering medium would be an ideal way to keep the oil clean. However, it is generally recognized that filtering also removes some of the beneficial additives from the engine oil, so the extent of filtering is questionable. Our recommendation is to change the oil filter at every recommended oil change (every 3,000 miles) and use the type (bypass or full-flow) specified by the manufacturer.

Engine oil must perform many jobs. It must reduce friction and resultant wear, keep the engine clean and free of oxidation and corrosion, act as a coolant, etc. It must do its job at high pressure and both high and low temperatures, and in an atmosphere polluted with dust, dirt, water, and contaminants caused by the combustion process. Oil is made up of many things to do many jobs, so pick a good one for many happy driving miles.

SUMMARY OF RECOMMENDATIONS

■ Use a national brand multiviscosity (multigrade) engine oil. 10-W30 or 10-W40 works for most conditions. Consider using a 5-W20 multigrade engine oil for cold-weather driving, typically below 0 degrees Fahrenheit.

■ Use an oil of performance classification SF.

■ Always use detergent-type engine oils.

■ Change the engine oil and filter at the same time—every 3,000 miles or sooner, especially with turbocharged cars that operate at higher temperatures, and for 4-cylinder cars that work harder than 6- or 8-cylinder cars.

MECHANIC'S TIPS

■ Clean the oil pan every 2 years or 25,000 miles. At that time inspect the oil pump screen and clean or repair as required. Also inspect the bearings at this time.

■ Drive at slow speeds and with light loads for at least the first 500 miles with a new car. The gray cast iron in the cylinders builds up a hard, glazed surface when under sliding friction. This glazing provides excellent wear resistance, and slow driving and light loads will facilitate the formation of this protective coating.

■ Don't use supplementary oil additives for normal driving. The oil manufacturer takes great precaution to include all the necessary additives and in the correct amounts and proportions. Considering our recommended oil change interval of 3,000 miles, buying cans of additive to supplement the oil is a waste of money. Exceptions: operation in an excessive idle mode or dusty environment.

■ Check the oil level at least once a week or at every fuel-up.

■ If your car is to be serviced by a mechanic, consider combining oil and filter changes with other service to save time and money.

■ Never overfill the crankcase when adding or changing oil. High oil levels can become diluted with gasoline and become thin enough to pass by the piston rings and burn in the cylinder, resulting in oil consumption. If the oil smells like gas, change it and the filter. High oil level can also rob the engine of horsepower by dragging against crankshaft counter-weights, and may also cause main engine seals to leak or blow out. Also, high oil level may be picked up by the crankcase venting system and end up in the air filter or carburetor, which could ruin the air cleaner element or clog small carburetor passages.

■ Use quality engine oil and filters; bargain products almost never save you money in the long run.

■ Never race the engine when starting up; allow oil pump to build pressure and circulate oil to all high friction areas. Racing an engine only improves the chance of developing a "knock" or noise in your car, and once you have a knock, it will cost you money to get rid of it.

■ Consider installing an engine oil cooler if you plan to do much heavy hauling or trailer towing.

■ Keeping your car tuned up will help prevent the engine oil from being diluted with gasoline.

■ If you change the oil yourself, always warm the engine to operating temperature first, then change the oil. This will help prevent the suspended dirt and deposits in the oil from clinging to the sides of the oil pan and contaminating the fresh oil. If you don't want to change the oil yourself, have your mechanic do it or take the car to a quick-change oil center. Most of these oil changes and lube businesses promise a 15-minute completion time. Just make sure they use the type of oil we recommend.

■ Combine car trips to save on gasoline and to make sure your engine warms to operating temperature. Driving on short trips for only a few miles will not rid the engine of harmful water vapor. Driving more miles will heat the engine to operating temperature, evaporate the water in the crankcase, and allow the vapor to be cleared by the ventilating system. Plan to drive at least 3 to 6 miles at a time in the summer and 10 to 14 miles in the winter for proper engine warm-up.

■ Change the oil more frequently than the 3,000 mile recommendation if you do a lot of short-trip driving.

4

Grease Lubrication

"CHANGE THE OIL AND GREASE IT" ARE INSTRUCTIONS A MECHANIC HEARS MANY TIMES during a week. Oil changes and grease jobs are undoubtedly two of the most common maintenance items performed on cars.

WHAT IS IT?

Grease is essentially a combination of a base mineral lubricating oil, as discussed in Chapter 3, and a thickening agent, such as a metallic soap. The many different types of greases are classified according to the soap base used (Table 4-1).

Synthetic grease is composed of the same types of metallic soaps, as stated above, but contains synthetic hydrocarbons instead of the usual base mineral oil. Synthetic greases are used in industry because of their ability to operate under a wide range of temperature.

Greases, just like lubricating oils, are available with additives. Additives, such as oxidation inhibitors and extreme-pressure additives are common. Filler materials such as mica, lead, zinc, carbon black, or graphite can be added to greases to enhance their lubricating ability. Normally, fillers are used to best advantage with extremely heavy loads or intermittent motion.

Classification is also made according to the application method. The National Lubricating Grease Institute (NLGI) has assigned NLGI consistency numbers to greases. This classification is shown in Table 4-2, along with methods of application.

The calcium soap-base grease listed in Table 4-1 is made by forming an emulsion of oil, soap, and water. Dehydration or loss of the water can occur in service or during long storage, especially when high temperatures are encountered. Excessive working

Table 4-1. Greases.

Metallic Soap Base	Structure	Operating Temperature	Operating Load	Application
Calcium (lime) soap	Smooth	160° F Max	Moderate	Wide speed ranges
Sodium (soda) soap	Fibrous	300° F Max	Wide range	
Aluminum soap	Salve-like	180° F Max	Moderate	
Lithium soap	Smooth	300° F Max	Moderate	Low temperature
Barium soap	Short fibers	350° F Max	Wide Range	Multipurpose

of the grease also tends to cause dehydration. For these reasons, the calcium soap-base grease is recommended where renewal of the grease is periodic (where new grease displaces the old grease), where working of the grease is not excessive, and where water is present. This grease might typically be used in steering linkages or suspension parts.

In sodium soap-base grease, water is not required to form the grease emulsion. It has a high melting point (400 degrees Fahrenheit), is soluble in water, and can withstand excessive working. This grease is used in high-temperature environments and where service is continuous, such as in roller bearings.

WHAT DOES IT DO?

In some applications, lubricating oils such as engine oil cannot be used because of their tendency to flow. Greases successfully overcome this difficulty. The metallic soaps mentioned above serve as the thickeners that act to keep the oil in place. Some of these thickeners have a lubricating quality of their own. However, it is actually the oil that is slowly released or bled from the grease that provides the bulk of the lubricating quality of the grease. When the oil has been depleted to 50% of the total weight of the grease, the lubricating quality of the grease is unreliable. This is one reason, along with the entrapment of dirt, that grease needs to be renewed periodically.

Table 4-2. NLGI Classification.

NLGI No.	Consistency	Application Method
0	Semifluid	Bush or gun
1	Very soft	Pin-type cup or gun
2	Soft	Pressure gun or
3	Light cup grease	pressure system
4	Medium cup grease	
5	Heavy cup grease	Pressure gun or hand
6	Block grease	Hand, cut to fit

Fig. 4-1. Front wheel bearing assembly.

In order to replenish this lost lubricating oil, bearings are supplied with an extra amount of grease in a reservoir or cavity close to the rolling element of the bearing. In a front wheel bearing assembly (Fig. 4-1), the hub cavity serves as this reservoir. Typical wheel bearing repacking instructions will include directions to put a glob of grease in the hub cavity. Care must be taken not to fill this cavity too full. Filling the cavity flush with both bearing races is the recommended limit. Excessive packing causes overheating, churning, and aerating, not to mention slippage of grease past the bearing seal and onto the brake lining. Follow the manufacturer's recommendations for application.

WHERE IS IT USED?

The front wheel bearings (on rear-wheel drive cars), the steering linkages, and the suspension parts are the major items that need periodic regreasing. Other parts include door, trunk, and hood hinges and latches, window slides, and various linkages and cables.

Wheel Bearings

Use only a specially formulated, fresh, clean wheel bearing grease for the front wheel bearings. Some manufacturers do not recommend using a fibrous-type grease. If so, follow their recommendation for grease type and NLGI classification. In the absence of a manufacturer's recommendation, we recommend using a good-quality sodium-, lithium-, or barium-based grease with an NLGI classification of 3. Remember to select one specially formulated for wheel bearings. Further, we recommend regreasing the front wheel bearings at the manufacturer's recommended interval or at every other oil change (every 6,000 miles), whichever is sooner.

Steering Linkages/Suspension Parts

These parts are not designed to experience high speed, intermittent loads, or high temperatures. They are exposed more than wheel bearings to water, ice, and snow, so take care to select an insoluble grease. Again, as for wheel bearings, follow the manufacturer's recommendations as to type. In the absence of other recommendations, use either the calcium- or aluminum-based grease of NLGI Nos. 2-4. Be sure the grease fittings are clean before regreasing. Perform this maintenance at the manufacturer's recommended interval or at every oil change (every 3,000 miles), whichever is sooner.

Universal Joints

All rear-wheel drive cars employ drive shafts that connect the transmission to the rear differential gears via two, and sometimes three, universal joints or U-joints. Some U-joints are lubricated for life at the factory and need no periodic lubrication. Others need to be lubricated periodically. You can tell if periodic lubrication of the U-joints is necessary by inspecting the U-joints for evidence of a grease fitting. If a grease fitting exists, then the U-joints must be regreased periodically. Follow the manufacturer's recommendations or regrease every other oil change (every 6,000 miles), whichever is sooner. In the absence of a recommendation of grease type, use a sodium or barium grease of NLGI No. 3 or 4.

WHITE GREASE

White grease is a light, lithium-based grease that is used to lubricate hinges, latches, linkages, and cables. It is creamy in color and texture. It will not wash away or dry out, and it also protects against rust and corrosion. It usually is bought in a small tube with a screw cap. To apply, simply squeeze the tube.

Lubricate door, hood, and trunk hinges and latches with white grease twice a year. Remember to clean the old grease completely before applying the new. It can also be used to lubricate cables and linkages such as those found on carburetors. Lubricate cables and linkages at their connection or termination points, and where they run through the fire wall or turn round a pulley. If your car has a standard transmission with the clutch activated by a clutch cable, follow this recommendation: use white grease at the termination points, but use a light grease with a graphite filler at the places the clutch cable rounds a pulley. The graphite particles will intersperse with the cable strands at these flexure points and provide marvelous lubrication.

MANUAL TRANSMISSION/REAR AXLE/STEERING GEAR BOX LUBRICANT

The manual transmission, the rear axle, and the steering gear are included in this chapter because these components use very viscous oils as lubricants. These oils are not greases, but the subject matter fits here.

Check the level of these lubricants at least twice a year, more often if any heavy or long-term towing is done. Lubricant levels should be maintained at the level of the threaded plug used to contain the lubricant. In no case should the lubricant level be more than ¼ to ½ inch below the threaded hole. If the lubricant level is low, add the manufacturer's specified type only. This is usually an SAE-80 or -90 multipurpose gear lubricant. For limited-slip axles a special lubricant with additives is required. Add lubricant with a gear lubricant syringe.

Change these lubricants yearly. Manual transmission lubricant can be changed by drawing out as much of the old lubricant as possible with a lubricant syringe before refilling with fresh lubricant. Rear axle lubricant change can be performed in the same manner. Look for a drain plug on the rear axle differential case, however, before proceeding with the syringe. If the case has a drain plug, drain the fluid by removing the plug. Refill by reinstalling the drain plug and adding the proper amount of fresh lubricant with the syringe. Follow the same procedure for the steering gear box.

SUMMARY OF RECOMMENDATIONS

■ Clean and grease wheel bearings every 6,000 miles. Use the factory-recommended grease type. If no recommendation is available, use a quality sodium-, lithium- or barium-based grease of NLGI No. 3 that is specially formulated for wheel bearings.

■ Regrease the steering linkages and suspension parts every 3,000 miles with the factory-recommended type grease. If no recommendation is available, use a calcium- or aluminum-based grease of NLGI Nos. 2-4.

■ Lube the U-joints (if they are the lubeable type) every 6,000 miles with the factory-recommended grease. If no recommendation is available, use a sodium or barium grease of NLGI No. 3 or 4.

■ Lubricate all door, hood, and trunk hinges and latches with white grease twice a year.

MECHANIC'S TIPS

■ Refer to the shop manual when performing a grease job to be sure to locate all the applicable grease fittings.

■ Don't mix grease types. Mixing two types of grease will impair the performance.

■ Inspect the old grease and transmission, axle, or steering gear lubricant for presence of any dirt or metal chips or filings.

■ Grease the car when the temperature of the fittings is above freezing. Joints will not accept grease when they are cold.

■ Always follow the factory-recommended methods when performing lube service.

■ Check for other lubrication areas in the shop manual and perform at those recommended intervals or sooner. If your plan is to perform them sooner, consider doing them twice as often as recommended in the shop manual.

■ The recommendations made in this chapter all boil down to one thing: if you get serious about lubrication of suspension and drive train components, you're bound to save a lot of money and aggravation. Tie-rod ends, ball joints, center links, and idler arms are not cheap when it comes time to replace them. Most of these repairs need to be done in a repair shop because of the special tools required to do the job right.

■ Wheel bearings, universal joints, and axle bearings that fail due to lack of lubrication not only cost plenty to repair but are often the cause of accidents. Wheels may lock up, causing loss of control of the vehicle, or drive shafts may fall out from under the car and jamb into the pavement or hit the car following you.

- Lubricate connection and termination points of linkages and cables twice a year with white grease. In the case of shift or clutch linkages, use a multipurpose molybdenum grease.
- Lubricate clutch cables, if applicable, twice a year with a light grease containing a graphite filler. Do this in the area where the cable rounds a pulley or goes through the fire wall.
- Check lubricant levels of the manual transmission, the rear axle, and the steering gear box at every oil change. Change these lubricants once a year with the factory-recommended types.

MECHANICS TIPS

- If hinges and linkages don't free up or respond to grease lubrication, try some penetrating oil to clean out old grease. Then lube with clean grease.
- Keeping your suspension parts lubricated and in good working order can save on tire wear and many times wear on the driver. It's no fun having to fight to keep your car on the road because of a worn-out front end. Again, consider the safety aspects of maintaining your car.
- Add only enough grease to a suspension joint to swell the rubber seal. Too much grease could break the seal, which must then be replaced. Joints that are not sealed should be lubricated until fresh grease appears at the joint edge.
- In cars designed with front-wheel drive, the axle drive or differential is located in the same housing as the manual transmission. These two components share the same lubricant. Check the lubricant level in the same manner as rear-wheel drive cars. If the front-wheel drive car has an automatic transmission, the two components will have separate lubricants and fill holes. Follow the recommendations in the shop manual.

5

Automatic Transmissions

AUTOMATIC TRANSMISSIONS ARE USED IN ALL SORTS OF VEHICLES: CARS, TRUCKS, BUSES, off-road heavy-duty vehicles, and sport vehicles. All automatic transmissions used on recent cars have the same general operating principles. All transmissions, manual and automatic, provide the means of selecting a forward or reverse direction for the car. Transmissions also provide combinations of speed and torque to start the car moving and keep it moving. These speed and torque ratio combinations provide the means to achieve the power, speed, and operating economy desired. Automatic transmissions perform most of the duties of the clutch and manual transmission automatically.

While all automatic transmissions in modern cars have the same general operating principles, parts of one type or manufacturer cannot usually be used in a transmission of another type or manufacturer. Automatic transmissions have hundreds of parts. Explaining the function of each is not our aim here. These parts can be arranged, however, into four major components or systems: the torque converter, the gear train, the hydraulic control system (HCS), and the transmission housing (Fig. 5-1).

TORQUE CONVERTER

The torque converter is mounted between the engine and the transmission gear train. The motion of the engine is transmitted via the rear end of the rotating crankshaft to the front of the torque converter assembly. Inside the torque converter this motion is transferred to the transmission gear train via a fluid connection or fluid coupling, rather than a mechanical connection or coupling (friction disc). The transmission fluid provides the means by which this fluid coupling can act. Stators and impellers inside the torque

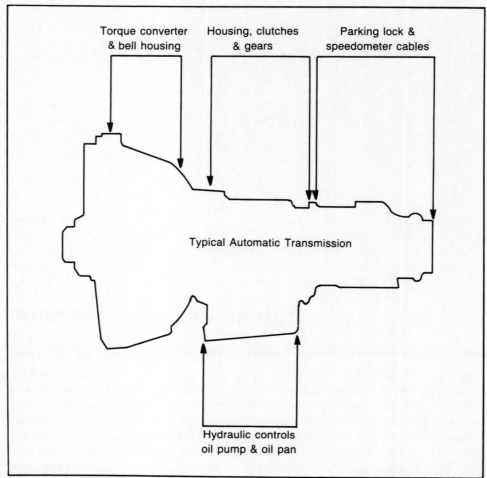

Torque converter
& bell housing

Housing, clutches
& gears

Parking lock &
speedometer cables

Typical Automatic Transmission

Hydraulic controls
oil pump & oil pan

Fig. 5-1. Automatic transmission.

converter assembly utilize the energy of the flowing transmission fluid to transmit rotational motion to the gear train. They act much like a windmill to change fluid flow energy to mechanical shaft energy.

The purpose of the torque converter, then, is to transmit engine torque from the engine to the transmission. The torque converter also increases engine torque and reduces speed as required, depending on operating demands. It absorbs drive train and engine torsional vibrations, acts as an automatic clutch, and smooths engine operation by acting as a flywheel.

The torque converter performs these many functions, normally without requiring routine service. Typically, a torque converter can last 100,000 miles or longer under ideal conditions. Poor driving habits and lack of proper service to other car systems that affect performance of the torque converter are responsible for most torque converter problems and result in short life.

Avoid putting the transmission into drive or reverse with the engine racing too fast. Try pumping the accelerator pedal to reduce idle speed when initially starting out. Also, avoid repeated shifts from reverse to drive and drive to reverse, as when stuck in snow or on a slippery surface. These shifts are frequently made too suddenly and at too high of an engine speed.

Tune the engine at regular intervals, being especially careful to adjust the engine idle speed to specification. Faulty engine performance and too high of an idle speed will have detrimental effects on the torque converter. Also, faulty engine cooling, damaged transmission oil cooler lines, or an overloaded engine or transmission (when towing) affect the life of the torque converter.

GEAR TRAIN

The gear train connects the torque converter to the drive shaft. It consists of a planetary gear set or sets and gear shafts. The gear train in an automatic transmission provides much the same services as the gear train in a manual transmission. Forward gears (two to four) are provided to match the forward speeds desired. A reverse speed gear (one only) is used to move the car in reverse. A neutral gear arrangement allows the engine to continue running while the car is stationary. Unlike manual transmissions, however, a park gear position is provided with automatic transmissions to prevent the car from moving when parked.

Gear trains in automatic transmissions are normally very reliable and provide long service. However, some wear is to be expected because of the relative movement of gear teeth. This wear is especially noticeable on the drive sides of the gear teeth since that is where the highest forces occur (Fig. 5-2). In addition, the gear train contains a number of bearings, bushings, and shafts that are also subject to wear.

Premature wear can be caused by low or high transmission fluid levels. Incorrect fluid levels can overheat the clutches and bands that act as holding devices to control gear operation (more about these components later). Overheating can cause failure of friction surfaces on clutches and bands, and can thin the fluid to a point where proper gear lubrication is lost. It seems obvious that dirt trapped within the transmission will cause premature wear of any close-fitting moving parts. This is a good reason to change the transmission fluid and filter often—perhaps every 25,000 miles, or sooner if towing heavy loads.

Transmission clutches and bands act as holding devices to control gear operation. Normally the bands are adjustable, so the discussion will focus on them. Bands are either rigid or flexible strips of material that are lined with a friction surface. This friction surface can be made from a relatively hard metallic coating or a soft organic material. The choice of surface coating depends on the gear operation it will affect. Metallic coatings are used on low and reverse gear bands, while the softer organic coatings are used on the faster-turning forward gear drums.

Bands are applied around gear drums by hydraulically controlled servopistons. The friction coating on the surface of the band keeps the gear drum from turning when the servo activates to tighten the band around the drum. The clearance between drum and band is crucial and is adjusted with an adjusting screw. This clearance should be checked and adjusted, if necessary, every time the transmission fluid is changed.

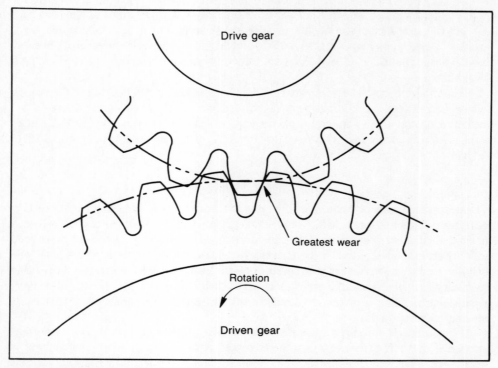

Fig. 5-2. Wear of gear teeth.

Use of the proper manufacturer's transmission fluid is absolutely necessary for proper band operation. Incorrect fluid will change the frictional characteristics between band and drum, causing subsequent changes in shifting characteristics. This is evidenced by harsher or delayed shifts. Damage can eventually result.

HYDRAULIC CONTROL SYSTEM

The hydraulic control system (HCS) delivers the transmission fluid at the correct location, pressure, and temperature to be used by the various transmission parts. The HCS provides fluid for the torque converter, provides the correct pressure to operate clutches and bands that control gear operation, and assures lubrication and cooling to all the torque converter and transmission parts.

The HCS consists of many parts and components, as listed below:

1. A reservoir or sump to contain the transmission fluid.
2. Pressure-regulating valves to maintain correct fluid pressure to various components.
3. Flow-control valves to regulate the correct amount of fluid to various components.
4. Hydraulic servos to operate clutches and bands.
5. Cushioning devices to prevent sudden and harsh clutch and band application.

6. A lube system to provide adequate transmission fluid to the various components needing lubrication.
7. A cooling system to guard against overheating.
8. Numerous seals and gaskets to contain the transmission fluid.
9. The transmission fluid itself.

The transmission fluid is the only part of the HCS that will be discussed in detail.

TRANSMISSION HOUSING

The transmission housing is the envelope that contains all the internal parts and components of the transmission. It consists of the bell housing for the torque converter, a case for the gear train and the HCS, the reservoir, and the extension housing for the transmission output shaft. It also provides the means to bolt the transmission to the car engine and frame.

In rear-drive cars the transmission and torque converter are attached to the rear of the engine. The drive shaft transmits the engine torque and motion to the rear axle. The differential, located in the rear axle, splits the drive to the two rear wheels. In front-drive cars the transmission, torque converter, and differential are mounted in one assembly in the front of the car, usually under or beside the engine. Open drive axles or half-shafts transmit the drive from the differential to the two front wheels. This arrangement is called a transaxle.

AUTOMATIC TRANSMISSION FLUIDS

Automatic transmission fluid (ATF) is nothing more than mineral oil of the correct viscosity with specially formulated additives. Viscosity index improver slows the rate of viscosity change in the fluid as temperature changes, just as with engine oil. Viscosity index improver additive improves transmission operation. Other additives include oxidation inhibitors and foam inhibitors. Foam inhibitors reduce entrapment of air in the ATF for effective operation of clutches and bands. Air entrapment can be caused by operating the transmission with incorrect fluid level. ATF and any additives must be compatible with all transmission materials, including steel, bronze, cast iron, aluminum, friction materials, and seal and gasket materials. A red dye is added to the ATF to distinguish transmission leaks from engine oil leaks.

Early ATF's were the same as engine oil. However, with the advent of bigger engines, air conditioning, and towing, heavier demands were placed on the transmission and fluid. Here's a brief history:

- Type A fluid—1949 GM, used in all automatic transmissions.
- Type A Suffix A—1957 GM, used to reduce varnish buildup.
- Type F—early 1960's, used for Ford transmissions only.
- Dexron—1968 GM, used with higher horsepower engines.
- CJ—1977 Ford, used with automatic overdrive transmissions.
- H—1977 Ford, used with Ford C5 transmission.
- Dexron II-D—current fluid for GM and some Chrysler and American Motors products.

The ATF is the means by which engine force and motion are transmitted to properly operate the transmission clutches, bands, servos, and valves. The ATF also cools and lubricates the various parts of the transmission, and makes a seal between moving parts. The clutches and bands with their friction coatings alone could not function without ATF; they would seize because of the tremendous heat of friction that would be quickly generated. The ATF provides, together with these friction coatings, the required frictional characteristics that will produce the desired slip-lockup of clutches and bands.

The ATF also transmits the engine torque to the torque converter and in turn to the clutches, bands, and gears. Tremendous heat is generated by this process and must be absorbed and dissipated to the atmosphere by the fluid in order to prevent overheating and subsequent damaging oxidation of the fluid.

ATF level changes with temperature and as a result of the varying needs of clutches and bands in different gear arrangements. Normal operating temperatures for transmission fluid are in the range of 175 to 185 degrees Fahrenheit. Use of air conditioning, stop-and-go traffic conditions, pulling heavy trailers, or rocking the car from forward to reverse repeatedly can cause overheating. Rocking a car can cause temperatures within the ATF to rise to 300 degrees Fahrenheit and beyond. If temperatures continue to rise, friction materials on clutches and bands can be destroyed. Avoid rocking a car with an automatic transmission; use another means to free up the car.

Time, temperature, overloading, and overuse take their toll on the transmission and fluid. With time, a buildup of burned friction materials from clutches and bands, and particles from cracked seals can foul the ATF. It's imperative to check the level and condition of the ATF periodically, especially under high-mileage operation. Check every 2 weeks; once a week if towing.

Check the ATF level at operating temperature, with the vehicle level, parking brake on, and gear selector lever in the factory-recommended position. Refer to the shop or owner's manual for interpretation of the fluid level markings found on the transmission dipstick. A low fluid level results in insufficient pressure to operate the clutches and bands. This causes slippage of the friction materials and overheating. A high fluid level will cause churning and foaming of the ATF. Foaming air is trapped in the ATF and is carried into the hydraulic control system. This, too, will cause clutch and band slippage and subsequent overheating.

The appearance of the ATF should be inspected on a clean, white cloth. Put a few drops on the fingers first. The ATF should feel smooth and slippery. Smell the fluid. If there is a burnt smell, the transmission might need servicing. Normally the ATF is pink in color. The fluid can be a light amber color but should not be a brown or dark color. Look for metallic particles or friction materials from clutches and bands. There shouldn't be any. A milky fluid indicates a coolant leak in the ATF via the fluid cooler in the radiator. It should be serviced immediately. Also check for any dark brown varnish deposits.

SUMMARY OF RECOMMENDATIONS

- Change transmission fluid and filter, and clean the pan every 25,000 miles with the recommended fluid. Do this about every 10,000 miles if towing a heavy load.
- Check and adjust the bands to specification at every fluid change.

- Use factory-recommended fluid only. Never substitute and *never* use engine oil in an automatic transmission.
- Maintain fluid at specified level. Never overfill. Check every 2 weeks or sooner.
- Never rock a car with an automatic transmission. Always shift casually, never suddenly from a forward gear to a reverse gear, and vice versa.
- Keep engine idle speed within specified limits. Check monthly.

MECHANIC'S TIPS

- Check and adjust the shift linkage and throttle linkage to specification at least once a year.
- Check and adjust the vacuum modulator system at least once a year.
- Check the exhaust gas recirculation system (EGR) at least once a year.
- Install after-market transmission oil cooler if doing heavy towing to ensure longer automatic transmission life.
- Servicing a transmission is many times less expensive than overhauling one. Most people never think of their transmission until it doesn't work.
- Never use dirty containers to store transmission fluid. Never use cans of transmission fluid that had been opened previously.
- When adding fluid to the automatic transmission, be sure the funnel is clean. Otherwise, you might be pouring in trouble instead of prolonging the life of your transmission.
- Use a lint-free rag to wipe the ATF dipstick. Lint will do more harm than dirt to the transmission.

6

Wear of Tires, Hoses, Belts and Other Rubber Parts

THERE ARE MANY PARTS IN THE CAR THAT EVENTUALLY FAIL BY SCRAPING OR RUBBING against other parts or surfaces. In fact, most of the parts that wear out in the car do so in this manner. This chapter presents the theory of wear and reviews the way that softer parts such as belts, hoses, and tires wear out.

THEORY OF WEAR

Failure of the surface of a part by wear usually occurs only after a very long time. For example, tires don't "wear out" in 1 day. Normally, tire wear occurs over years (or many miles) of use and is characterized by shallow tread depth. For example, a flat tire caused by a puncture from a nail or sharp glass cannot be classified as a wear failure. Wear failure takes a relatively long time to occur. There are three principal types of wear at work in the car: adhesive, abrasive, and pitting wear.

Adhesive Wear

There is no surface made by man that is perfectly smooth. All surfaces, even the smoothest, have some surface markings, which are especially evident under a microscope. Many rough peaks and valleys come into focus. The roughness peaks act as points of adhesion. As two surfaces slide over each other, wear will occur because of the grinding and plucking away of material at these points of adhesion. Piston rings, camshaft surfaces, and improperly lubricated bearings, for example, can wear in this manner.

Abrasive Wear

When a hard, rough surface slides against a softer one, abrasive wear can occur. An excellent example of abrasive wear is the effect of sandpaper on wood. The abrasive particles on the sandpaper are very hard and rough, while the surface of the wood is much softer. The sandpaper particles actually plough a series of grooves, removing wood material with each stroke. Another example of abrasive wear is when hard, rough particles are introduced between sliding surfaces (as in dirt in journal bearings). Tire wear is also abrasive wear. A hard, rough road surface is responsible for tire wear, acting on the tire just like sandpaper acts on wood. The reason tires last as long as they do is that the relative motion between the tire and road is not only a sliding motion but a rolling motion as well, and the rolling motion does not contribute as significantly to tire wear as sliding motion does.

Pitting Wear

Pitting is caused by the surface failure of a material as a result of repeated surface stresses that exceed the strength of the material. Pitting stops when these stresses become less than the strength of the material. Pitting is a common mode of failure for gear teeth. Usually poor design is responsible for this type of wear.

TIRES

The air used to inflate tires must support the total weight of a car, plus passengers and cargo. In addition, tires and the air used to inflate them control stopping, turning, and smoothness of ride. As we will see, insuring proper tire inflation is one of the most important steps that can be taken to prolong tire life and help guarantee satisfactory and safe performance.

Construction

Tires are constructed of rubber, fabric, and steel. On the inside, tires are made of a tough fabric that is reinforced with steel threading to add strength. All the components are molded on a heated form. The heat vulcanizes the rubber to make it more resistant to wear. Vulcanization is a toughening process used for many different rubber products. Tires consist of four basic parts: the body, bead, cord, and tread (Fig. 6-1).

The body (or sidewall) acts to help support the weight of the car. It must be properly inflated so that it is stiff enough to bounce back from various road shocks and yet flexible enough to provide a comfortable ride. As with other parts of the tire, it must also be abrasion-resistant.

The function of the tire bead is to hold the tire securely against the wheel rim to prevent air leakage. The bead is constructed of rings of steel wire that prevent the inside diameter of the tire from stretching because of air pressure and centrifugal rotational force. All tires have bead gauges molded to the body to show proper tire seating to the wheel rim. The distance between the edge of the wheel rim and the bead gauge should be even all around the rim (Fig 6-2).

Cords provide the material of the body wall and a mounting surface for the tread. They are made from various materials including nylon, rayon, polyester, glass-fiber, and

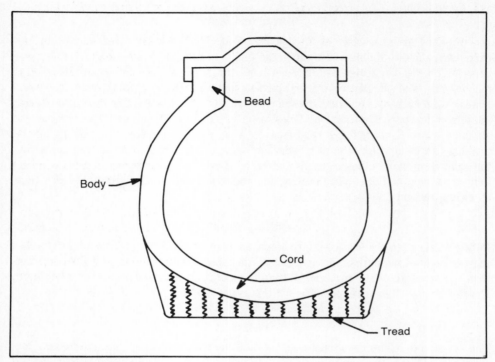

Fig. 6-1. Anatomy of a tire.

Fig. 6-2. Tire bead gauge.

steel. Each has its own advantages of ride comfort, abrasion resistance, and resistance to road damage.

The tire tread is the part of the tire that grips the road. It permits the tire to roll smoothly along the road and must take on a variety of surfaces. The tread is made almost entirely of synthetic rubbers, with the addition of sulfur and carbon black to harden the rubber. Tread designs vary greatly, with no one design proven superior. Choose a tread design to match driving conditions or for general use. Some of the newer tread designs can be used for a combination of driving conditions.

Types

There are three major types of tires, classified by the way the cords are molded into the tire and the use of belts in the tread area. These are bias-ply, belted bias-ply, and radial ply. We will only discuss radial-ply tires here.

In a radial-ply tire, the body cords are molded from bead to bead at 90 degrees to the tire diameter. Bias-ply tires have the cords molded at angles between 30 and 38 degrees. Running the cords at 90 degrees in the radial-ply tire results in a very rigid tread, but a flexible sidewall or body—giving superior road handling quality and longer wear. If you can afford them, radial-ply tires are the best choice.

Caution: Use radial-ply tires in sets of four. Never mix radials with non-radials. If you change to snow tires in the winter, buy radial-ply snow tires if you are using radial-ply tires on the other axle. Using different types of tires results in different types of traction, which can lead to dangerous handling problems.

Care

Tires probably require more care than any other part on a car. Tires not only support the weight of the car, they do many other jobs depending on whether they are located on the front or rear axle. Tires on front-wheel drive cars must perform all of the work of the front axles, plus many of the jobs of the rear wheels as well.

Rotation. Front wheels steer the car, absorb misalignment irregularities, and are more subject to braking wear than the rear wheels. Rear wheels drive or push the car, hold the car on curves, and absorb sudden stops and starts. The different kinds of work these tires perform result in different kinds of wear. In order to maximize tire life and equalize wear on all tires, they should be rotated at regular intervals as specified by the manufacturer. In the absence of a manufacturer's recommendation, rotate the tires every 12,000 miles according to the pattern in Figs. 6-3 and 6-4.

Make sure the wheel and tire are properly balanced at this interval. Note that radial, belted bias-ply, and studded winter tires should not be rotated. Radial and belted bias-ply tires are to be switched from front to rear or vice-versa. They must always rotate in the original wheel positions as when first installed. These tires, because of their construction, acquire a sort of "permanent set" that will adversely affect performance if you reinstall them in different positions.

Storage. Store tires in a clean, dry area away from tools. Don't pile other storage items on tires. Lay the tires flat, if possible, on an oil-free floor. Tires can also be stored in a rack and stood on the tread.

Inflation. The most important thing you can do to prolong the life of car tires is to keep them properly inflated. Check tire pressure once per month when tires are cold

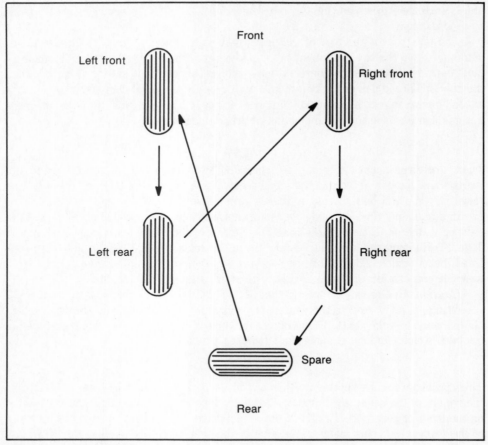

Fig. 6-3. Tire rotation—with spare tire.

and more often in winter because cold weather causes tire pressure to decrease. Remember that every 10-degree Fahrenheit temperature drop will decrease tire pressure by 1 psi.

Every mechanic has a recommendation for proper tire inflation. Some of them even recommend different inflation pressures to match differing circumstances, such as winter driving or driving on a long trip. This is simply not true. Always keep them inflated according to manufacturer's specifications.

Low tire pressure will cause the tread to slip and scuff on the shoulders. It also reduces the stiffness of the sidewall, leading to excessive flexure and overheating. Overheating will cause accelerated wear and, on older tires, sudden failure.

High tire pressure is equally undesirable. It causes center wear in the tread and overstrains the sidewall, making it more susceptible to fabric breaks. Keep the pressure at the recommended level.

Cleaning. Clean the tire treads anytime you notice embedded nails, stones, or pieces of metal or glass. These items can lead to tire leaks and punctures, and will accelerate tread wear. In extreme cases they could lead to diminished tire traction.

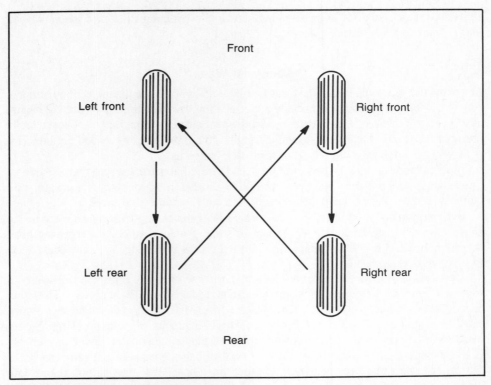

Fig. 6-4. Tire rotation—without spare tire.

If new whitewall tires are purchased, they normally come with a protective coating on the whitewalls. Remove this coating at the dealer or soon after. Remove road dirt on whitewalls with soap and water only. Never use gasoline or kerosene because they deteriorate the rubber and will discolor the whitewall.

Keep the tire valves clean. They must have valve caps to help keep dirt, water—and in winter, ice—out of the valve core.

Normal Wear

All tires, even on the best-maintained cars, will eventually wear out. The key to normal tire wear is to diminish the sliding effects (or sliding friction) and accentuate the rolling effects (or rolling friction) of the tire against the road. As we pointed out previously, sliding of one surface over another results in more wear than rolling motion between two surfaces. In fact, sliding wear on passenger car tires is estimated to be 90 to 100 times greater than rolling wear.

Normal tire wear results from a combination of rolling and sliding friction. Every time you round a curve, sliding friction increases. Every time you start or stop your car, sliding friction increases. Every time sliding friction increases, tire wear rates increase. If we could all drive on straight roads and start and stop gradually, we could keep rolling friction dominant over sliding friction. Therefore, driving habits are a prominent force in the fight for longer tire life. Slow down on curves and avoid quick stops and "jack-rabbit" starts. Keep the sliding to a minimum! Rolling friction will still cause wear; but it is far less severe.

Abnormal Wear

Abnormal tire wear can be due to a number of conditions or combinations of conditions. The more damaging conditions include underinflation, overinflation, poor driving habits, misaligned front wheels, out-of-balance wheels, bent suspension parts, out-of-round brake drums, brakes out of adjustment, and driving on rough roads for extended periods. Refer to Fig. 6-5 for recognizable abnormal wear patterns.

Overinflation causes the center of the tread to wear at a greater rate than the edges. Conversely, underinflation will cause the edges of the tread to wear at a greater rate than the center. Again, keep tire pressure at the recommended level.

Driving too fast around curves and corners is evidenced by tread worn more at the edges than the center, along with a rounded tread profile. Another poor driving habit is jerky braking. A tire will exhibit a saw-toothed profile at the edges of individual treads from jerky braking habits.

Misalignment of the front wheels is a major cause of rapid, abnormal tire wear. In some extreme, uncorrected cases, tire life can be reduced to 10% of normal. Tires that hiss or squeal while in operation may indicate incorrect toe-in. You might also notice small feather-edges at one side of an individual tread that point to toe-in problems. Spotty tread wear or tread with only one side worn can indicate incorrect caster or camber. Uneven tread wear can also be indicative of out-of-balance wheels, out-of-round brake drums, or brakes that need adjusting. Correct these problems immediately, then rotate the tires according to the patterns in Figs. 6-3 and 6-4 to help even out the tire wear.

Wheel Balancing

As pointed out above, an out-of-balance wheel can cause abnormal tire wear. Unbalanced wheels can set up violent vibrations that not only contribute to abnormal tire wear, but result in handling and braking problems. Balancing the wheel equally distributes the weight of the wheel, brake drum, hub, and tire around the center of the axle or axis of rotation.

There are two ways a wheel can be unbalanced: statically and dynamically. You can tell static unbalance by a pounding action of the wheel sometimes called "wheel tramp." A wobble or shimmy of the wheel is an indication of dynamic unbalance. Check wheel balance after every wheel or tire repair, at the time snow tires are installed, or twice per year. Missing balance weights also signal the time to rebalance. And remember that, although the front wheels are more sensitive to unbalance, all four wheels should be balanced both statically and dynamically.

HOSES

Rubber hose is used throughout the car to do a number of jobs. It always acts as a conduit to convey liquids or gases to various locations. Heater hoses convey hot engine coolant to the car heater/defroster for our comfort in cold weather. Radiator hose delivers cooled liquid to keep the engine running without overheating. Brake hose supplies high-pressure hydraulic or brake fluid to the wheel cylinders to stop the car, and acts to absorb surges

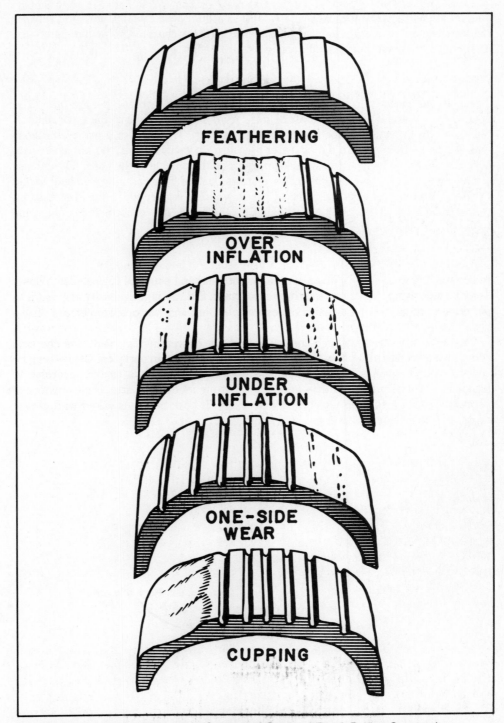

FEATHERING

OVER INFLATION

UNDER INFLATION

ONE-SIDE WEAR

CUPPING

Fig. 6-5. Abnormal tire wear patterns (Courtesy of Goodyear Tire & Rubber Company).

and vibrations between car body and wheels. Vacuum hose contains low-pressure air that can be used to operate the vacuum advance on the carburetor, a vacuum-controlled fuel pump, or vacuum-concealed headlights.

Parts

There are three parts to a hose: (Fig. 6-6) the cover, the carcass, and the tube. The cover protects the internal parts of the hose from harmful effects of the environment. It is made from natural rubber or a synthetic rubber. The carcass provides the hose with the strength to resist bursting under pressure. In vacuum hose, the carcass resists collapse due to the higher atmospheric pressure on the outside of the hose. The carcass can be made from fabric plies, fiber or wire braids, knitted fiber yarns, woven fiber yarns, or wire. The tube conveys the liquid or gas to where it is needed. It must be resistant to the liquid inside it and must not contaminate the liquid. It is constructed of the same types of materials as the cover.

Failure

In general, there are only a few major causes of wear and eventual failure in auto hose. They include aging, puncture, improper installation and routing; excessive exposure to oil, grease, or gasoline; excessive exposure to ozone; and workmanship errors (Table 6-1).

All hose will eventually age and fail as a result of weathering, heat, and chemical action. Keep all fluids that flow in hose clean and free of foreign particles. Change engine coolant yearly. Make sure that when new hose is installed, it is routed according to manufacturer's recommendation—keep it away from hot engine parts. Wipe down hose periodically with a soft rag moistened with water. If hose becomes caked with grease or oil, use a cleaner that will not attack the hose.

Fig. 6-6. Parts of a hose.

Table 6-1. Hose Failures and Their Causes.

Symptom	Cause	Cure
1. Hose tube hard and cracked.	Heat that leaches plasticizers* out of the tube. Also, too much air in tube.	Eliminate overheating. Eliminate air leaks.
2. Cover deteriorated.	Battery acid, steam cleaners, salt water, chemical cleaners, oils, greases, gasoline.	Reroute hose or protect during engine cleaning.
3. Burst hose on outside bond.	Use of less than recommended bend radius.	Reroute hose.
4. Burst hose; appears kinked and flattened.	Twisting of hose during installation.	Install hose without twisting.
5. Burst hose. Hose deteriorated with surface crazed.	Old age caused by weathering and ozone.	Replace hose at regular intervals. Do not park car around electrical equipment (motors) that produce ozone.

*Plasticizers add flexibility to hose.

Inspect hose according to the following list.

1. Replace cracked, swollen, restricted, or punctured hose.
2. Hose should be firm but not hard. Hardness indicates imminent failure.
3. Make sure hose clamps are not installed overly tight. A too-tight hose clamp can cut the hose cover and lead to premature failure.
4. Radiator hose normally has a steel wire wound within the hose material or placed inside the hose. Its function is to keep the radiator hose inside diameter fully open, ensuring proper coolant flow. The radiator hose should not feel soft or mushy. Replace accordingly.
5. Don't forget to check the radiator overflow tube. If it becomes clogged, cooling system venting will be impaired and cause radiator damage. Replace or clean accordingly.
6. Check brake hose whenever brake service is performed or whenever the car is on a lift. Check for cracks, worn spots, and interference with chassis or wheel parts. If replacement is warranted, use only approved replacement hose.

BELTS

Almost all cars make use of belts to transmit power from the crankshaft to auxiliary engine equipment such as fans, water pumps, power steering pumps, alternator/generator equipment, and air-conditioning compressors. These belts are normally V-shaped in cross-section and, hence, are called V-belts. V-belts ride in pulleys with V-shaped grooves. The V-belt should ride with its top surface approximately flush with the top of the pulley groove. Clearance must exist between the bottom of the V-belt and the bottom of the pulley groove to allow the V-belt to ride on the walls of the pulley groove.

V-belts are made of fabric fashioned into a cord impregnated with rubber. The cord material can be made of cotton, synthetic materials, or steel.

Another belt used in modern cars is the cogged V-belt, which replaces the chain belt used for timing purposes. In our opinion, this design use of rubberized belting is a poor one. These timing belts frequently break, rendering the car immobile. They are expensive and difficult to replace. If your car uses a rubber belt for timing purposes, inspect it frequently for wear and/or damage.

There are only a few things you can do to ensure long belt life. Check the condition of the belt periodically, say monthly. Cracked, brittle, glazed, or worn belts must be replaced as soon as possible. Check the belt tension periodically with a belt tension gauge. A loose belt can cause the water pump to run slowly and can lead to overheating problems. It can also lead to premature battery failure by allowing the alternator to slip, thereby slowly draining the battery. Don't try to adjust the belt tension by feel: in modern cars this method is not accurate enough. Use a belt tension gauge to set correct tension, as specified by the shop manual.

For a V-belt to properly do its job and last a long time, it must also run tightly in the pulley groove. If the belt slips it will squeak and wear prematurely. Usually a few drops of belt lubricant on the inside edges of the belt will stop the squeaking and prevent the belt from slipping. Be sure the belt is properly adjusted before using the V-belt lube.

OTHER RUBBER PARTS

Rubber or rubber-like parts are used throughout the car. Doors, trunks, and hoods all have rubber gaskets to keep out the weather. Inspect these at least yearly. They can be lubed with spray-on silicon.

Trunk and engine hoods may also have rubber bumpers to absorb road vibrations and the force from slamming them shut. Replace them if they are missing, cracked, or broken.

Cars that have separate frames and bodies use rubber bumpers at certain places between the frame and body to absorb vibrations. Find their location in your car by referring to the shop manual, and inspect them yearly. Replace as required. Unibody cars might not have these rubber bumpers.

Shock absorbers use rubber bushings in the mounting arrangement. Check these yearly for cracking. You can buy replacement bushings without buying new shock absorbers. The cost is less than a dollar and the improvement in ride, handling, and safety is well worth it.

Check the condition of the rubber filler hose between the gasoline fill port and gasoline tank yearly or every time the car is on the lift. A hard, cracked, or worn hose needs to be replaced. This hose is made of rubber to absorb the differential movement between the car body and gas tank.

SUMMARY OF RECOMMENDATIONS

- Check for proper tire inflation weekly.
- Buy radial bias-ply tires at replacement time. Don't mix radials with other type tires.

- Rotate tires periodically—every 12,000 miles or yearly.
- Clean tire treads periodically, about every 2 weeks.
- Balance tires when repairs are made, when changing to snow tires, when wheel weights are missing, or twice per year.
- Improve driving habits to lengthen tire life: slow down on curves and corners, and eliminate "jack-rabbit" starts and stops.
- Change engine coolant yearly to improve the life of radiator and heater hoses.
- Inspect brake hose when brake service is performed or when the car is on the lift for any other service. Replace accordingly.
- Inspect rubber belting monthly. Replace or adjust as necessary.
- Inspect miscellaneous rubber parts at least yearly.

MECHANIC'S TIPS

Tires

- Always use a quality tire—radials if possible. Be sure the tire is suited for type of vehicle and the conditions under which it is used—for example, snow, all-terrain, or all-season tires. Tires are designed for various applications.
- Follow manufacturer's suggestions on inflation and rotation of tires for longer tire life and safer driving.
- Check alignment and balance if tires begin to wear in an abnormal pattern.
- Never mix tire sizes or tire types on the same axle; this could be dangerous under certain conditions.

Hoses and Belts

- When replacing hoses of any type, always use the proper hose for each application and be sure it is a quality brand name. Never substitute an incorrect hose to make a permanent repair, or to cut cost of repairs.
- Check hoses for cracks and splits—signs of age and possible failure. Never check radiator hoses when system is hot or under pressure.
- Hoses and belts should be replaced every 3 years, even if they seem to be in good shape. The insides of hoses or undersides of belts are often not inspected the way they should be.
- Be certain to replace belts with proper sizes and width—as manufacturer suggests.
- Do not overtighten belts—not only will the belt wear out before it should, but many times the bearings in the component being driven by the over-tightened belt will fail from overloading in one direction.
- Check all rubber parts more often than you think you need to. Many times a faulty hose or belt is overlooked; and this same hose or belt could be the culprit when you find yourself broken down in the middle of nowhere.

7

Shocks, Mufflers, and Brakes

IN CHAPTER 6 WE DISCUSSED THE WEARING OF PARTS MADE PRIMARILY FROM RUBBER. IN this chapter, we will focus on the wearing of parts made from metals. Also included is wearing of brake discs and shoes.

SHOCK ABSORBERS

The combination coil spring and shock absorber that is found on the wheel of the car is actually part of the suspension system. The spring, not the shock absorber, is the component that actually absorbs road shocks. The job of the shock absorber is to dampen or "still" the many vibrations the spring makes as it absorbs shocks caused by road conditions and to hold the wheel to the road.

You can test for weak shock absorbers by bouncing the car while parked. The car body should bounce only once or twice. If the car doesn't "settle down" after one or two hard bounces, the shocks might be weak. Some cars have the spring and shock absorber combined into a single, replaceable unit called a McPherson strut. Also, many Chrysler products do not use coil springs on the front suspension, but use torsion bars instead. Torsion bars absorb road shocks by twisting.

The larger the shock absorber, the more fluid it has inside it. The more fluid it has, the more spring energy it can absorb. Larger shocks normally work at lower pressures for longer life. Heavy-duty shocks have more fluid than standard-duty shocks, so they will last longer for only a slightly higher cost. Use only the heavy-duty type shock sized for your car. Table 7-1 lists the four types of shock absorbers and their characteristics.

Table 7-1. Types of Shock Absorbers.

Type	Driving Conditions	Ride	Replacement
Standard duty	Normal speeds on well-paved roads. No heavy loads.	Soft	Often
Heavy duty	Rough roads at high speeds. Some towing or heavy loads	Firm but not hard	Less often than standard duty.
Spring type or load-leveling	Heavy loads or frequent towing	May be hard	About as often as heavy duty
High performance	High speed driving as in police cars	Firm to uncomfortable	Long life

Wear

Shock absorbers are factory-filled with an exact amount of fluid (liquid or gas), then sealed shut. They cannot be refilled, and there is no service that can be performed on the shock absorber itself to increase its life. Once worn, shocks need to be replaced.

A shock absorber can wear out in one of two ways. First, it can develop a leak. This becomes evident when oil moisture is noticed on the outside of the shock absorber. We advise replacing immediately. Second, the piston rod of the shock absorber can become scratched during installation or from a buildup of abrasive road dirt. This can cause premature wear of the piston rod seals, and subsequent internal seal failure. Eventually, you will notice a mushy ride and possible external leakage around the shock body. Other than factory defects or damage due to accidents, these are the only two ways shocks fail.

In Chapter 6 we pointed out that the rubber shock bushings located at the mounting locations on the shock can wear out. Again, check for loose or cracked bushings. Replace as required.

Replace worn shock absorbers in complete sets of four. Replacing only front or rear shocks can result in a rocking or pitching ride because the old shocks will not equalize reaction to bumps with the new. Even from the best set of shocks, expect a lifetime of only 25,000 to 30,000 miles. Normally the wearing process of these many miles is so gradual it's hard to notice. Our suggestion is to replace all the shocks at 25,000 miles, regardless—or sooner if they leak or exhibit weakness before then. This is most important in improving tire life, because a weak shock will allow the wheel to spin when rebound is not controlled. More importantly, weak or worn shocks are dangerous because they make it difficult to control a bouncing car.

Tips for Longer Shock Life

Periodic checking of bushings to verify tightness of installation is one way to keep shock absorbers lasting longer; improving driving habits is another. Here is a list of some things you might try.

47

1. Cut down on high-speed cornering.
2. If possible, avoid rough, bumpy roads.
3. Come to a gradual stop; never stop so quickly (unless in an emergency) that the car pitches front violently.
4. Distribute passengers and loads evenly throughout the car as much as possible.
5. Install shocks designed for frequent towing or heavy loads if you perform such functions often.
6. Never grip the piston rod with pliers or dirty hands. It is highly polished, and any scratches or dirt will accelerate internal seal wear.
7. Never extend a shock while it is upside down or lying on its side. Air can enter the shock in this way and cause a weak, mushy ride.
8. Slow down when crossing obstacles such as potholes or railroad tracks. This will lessen the spring energy the shock must absorb.

THE EXHAUST SYSTEM

In an internal combustion engine, fuel burns inside the cavity created by the cylinder walls and the moving piston. The fuel burns very rapidly in order to keep the piston and crankshaft assembly moving at a speed suitable to match driving conditions. In fact, the fuel burns so fast that you can think of it as exploding up to 16,000 times per minute. These explosions can be compared to a firecracker going off; they make noise. Each explosion in the cylinder generates a sound wave at least 50 feet long, with pulsations 20 to 250 times a second at high exhaust gas velocity. It falls upon the muffler and resonator (if so equipped) to quiet this noise.

Mufflers and resonators work by decreasing the exhaust gas velocity and by absorbing the sound waves (in special materials within the muffler), or canceling them by interference with other sound waves from the engine. To help decrease the exhaust gas velocity, mufflers should have volumes six to eight times the piston displacement. Most mufflers and resonators contain baffles, with or without holes to absorb sound and cancel sound waves. Also, some mufflers split the exhaust gas flow into two paths, having it meet again out of phase before leaving the tailpipe, thus canceling it out.

Mufflers and resonators are part of the exhaust system which, in addition, is composed of the exhaust manifold and connecting pipes and pipe hangers. Single exhaust passenger cars include an exhaust pipe, muffler, resonator (if so equipped), and a tailpipe that discharges exhaust gases at the rear of the car. An exhaust crossover pipe may be used on V-8 model cars to connect the two exhaust manifolds.

On dual-exhaust systems (available on V-8 models only), two assemblies consisting of exhaust manifolds, mufflers, resonators, and tailpipes are used. Each assembly is connected to its own exhaust manifold. On modern cars, a catalytic converter is also part of the exhaust system. This is an emission-control device used to reduce hydrocarbon, carbon monoxide, and oxides of nitrogen pollutants from the exhaust gas. The catalyst used in converters eventually wears out or clogs from oil emissions in the exhaust gas. Some types of catalyst are replaceable, those in bead-type converters, for example. The bead-type converters are normally flat or pan-shaped. Monolith converters, using irreplaceable catalysts, are usually more tubular, and when the catalyst wears out, the entire converter assembly must be replaced (Figs. 7-1 and 7-2).

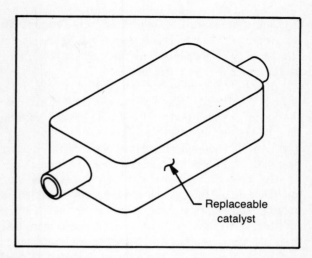

Fig. 7-1. Bead-type catalytic converter.

Replaceable catalyst

There are two types of catalysts. The conventional oxidation catalyst is made from platinum and palladium, and acts on hydrocarbon and carbon monoxide pollutants. It is sometimes called a two-way catalyst. The second type of catalyst, called a three-way catalyst, controls oxide of nitrogen, as well as hydrocarbon and carbon monoxide pollutants. The catalyst that controls oxides of nitrogen is made from rhodium and platinum.

Normal Wear

The life of exhaust system parts is dependent largely on the type of driving done. Short trips of 3 to 6 miles duration—especially in colder weather—or a lot of stop-and-go driving can rust the muffler and perhaps the tailpipe, too, in as little as 20,000 miles. On cars that have dual-exhaust systems, muffler and tailpipe life can be far less than 20,000 miles for this type of driving.

The reason for such short life is that on short trips, condensed moisture from the exhaust gas collects in the mufflers and pipes. In fact, for each gallon of gasoline, almost

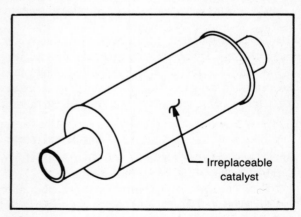

Fig. 7-2. Monolith catalytic converter.

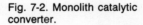
Irreplaceable catalyst

1 gallon of acidic water is generated by the engine. The exhaust system might not have enough time to heat up and evaporate this moisture. Because the moisture is highly acidic, it will rapidly corrode metal. Mufflers are particularly susceptible to this corrosion because of their complex and thin insides.

If you are forced to drive on short trips or in city stop-and-go traffic, then the above wear is considered normal for your car. Expect to replace exhaust system parts frequently. As much as possible, try to combine several short trips into one longer trip in order to give the exhaust system more time to rid itself of moisture. An excellent idea is to purchase a lifetime-guaranteed muffler at replacement time. No matter how many mufflers wear out, they will be replaced free of charge.

As pointed out above, if the car is driven on longer trips (over 6 miles in summer or 10 in winter), the exhaust system parts should get hot enough to evaporate the exhaust moisture. Exhaust system parts will last much longer as corrosive action is reduced. In addition, exhaust system parts will last longer on single-exhaust systems as opposed to dual-exhaust systems, because all exhaust gases must pass through a single muffler and pipes. As a result, the exhaust system will reach high temperature more quickly and the acidic moisture will evaporate sooner.

Normal wear, even on longer trips, is still a result of the corrosive action of the acidic exhaust moisture on metal parts, but exhaust system parts last very much longer. Mufflers and tailpipes (the last system parts to warm up), can last to 60,000 miles under these conditions. If you are getting this kind of life from exhaust parts, there is really nothing you can do to increase it. Just be sure to invest in a lifetime guarantee muffler at replacement time.

Other normal wear consists of loose, broken, or misaligned clamps, hangers, shields, and brackets. If any of these exist, check the exhaust system parts and make sure everything is properly aligned. Adjust or replace parts as necessary.

Anytime the car is on a lift for service, or the car rattles or hisses from underneath, inspect the entire exhaust system. Inspect the pipes, catalytic converters, mufflers, and resonators for cracked joints, broken welds, or corrosion damage that causes leaks. Make sure the clamps and hangers are in good shape. The bolt threads should not be corroded or stripped, and insulators should not be cracked. A good bet is to replace clamps and hangers when they are loosened, or if they have been on the car for more than 3 years. Use special care when inspecting the exhaust system or working on it; wait until it cools down.

Try jabbing at rusted areas with a screwdriver. If you go through the metal, replace the part. Also, try tapping the parts of the exhaust system. The metal is in good shape if you hear a ringing sound. A dull sound might mean the part is corroded. Jiggle the exhaust parts and inspect for movement. The entire system should move as one integrated part. Individual joints should not flex; adjust them if they do.

Abnormal Wear

Abnormal wear of the exhaust system is caused by either road damage, excessive oil burning, or an engine badly out of time.

Road damage can be caused by any number of things. Driving at high speeds over rough roads can cause the exhaust system parts to jar out of adjustment. Also, small stones can penetrate already corrosion-weakened metal parts. Drive slowly and cautiously if you encounter hazardous road conditions.

Excessive oil burning is a primary reason for premature catalytic converter failure. Converters can become clogged with oil and/or burned oil to the point that the car will not operate because the exhaust gases can't get through the system. Most of the time, unfortunately, this problem goes uncorrected because fixing the oil consumption problem can be costly, especially if new piston rings are needed. However, by following the recommended oil change interval in Chapter 3, excessive oil burning will probably never occur. In older cars that already burn oil, decide whether the repairs are warranted from a cost viewpoint. In any case, don't let this condition continue. Oil burning will not only clog the converter, but it is a foul condition that pollutes the air.

An engine that is badly out of tune will pass a number of things along to the exhaust system that the system is not designed to handle. Worn spark plugs and carburetion problems may result in incomplete combustion and subsequently introduce unburned gasoline into the exhaust system. Timing out of specification can send unburned gasoline through the exhaust system, as well as subject it to shocks it is not designed to handle. Clogged air filters may result in breathing restrictions for the engine, with loss of adequate flow through the exhaust system. This could accentuate condensation problems. Keep the engine in tune by following our recommendations in Chapters 8, 9, and 10.

BRAKES

Aside from the steering, the brake system is the most vital safety system on the car. We couldn't slow down or stop without it. Brakes work by friction—in fact, the brake on each wheel is simply a friction-generated, heat machine. When the car is brought to a stop, the slipping of the brake shoe friction material against the wheel generates heat. The amount of heat varies according to the weight of the car and the square of the speed. The faster the car is traveling and the heavier the load in the car, the more heat is generated to bring the car to a stop. If the speed of the car is doubled, four times the heat is generated to stop the car.

Types of Brakes and Brake Systems

All modern cars use essentially two types of brakes: the internal expanding shoe type or the disc brakes. Some cars combine these types, typically using disc brakes on the front wheel and shoe brakes on the rear wheels.

The internal expanding shoe brake (Fig. 7-3) consists of the wheel, two shoe assemblies, various springs and retaining devices, and a wheel cylinder. As shown on the illustration, the wheel cylinder supplies the needed actuating forces (F). The shoe assemblies are lined with a friction material commonly made of molded asbestos that is glued or riveted to the metal shoe.

As you apply the brake pedal, hydraulic pressure causes the wheel cylinder to expand its two pistons against the brake shoe at (F). This force throws the shoe (actually the friction surface of the shoe) against the inner surface of the wheel. The angular velocity of the wheel is gradually changed to heat energy as the car slows down.

An important feature of this type of brake is the self-energizing capacity of brake shoe (A). For the wheel rotation noted, when the wheel cylinder applies the force (F)

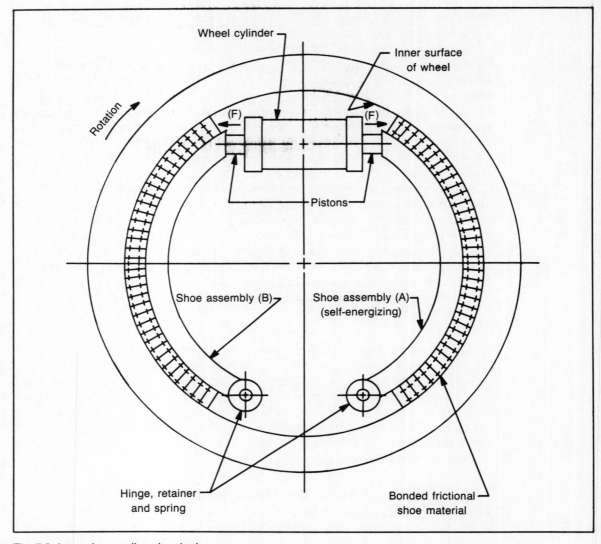

Fig. 7-3. Internal expanding shoe brake.

to brake shoe (A), the shoe is drawn into the moving wheel much as a magnet draws a piece of steel to it. Therefore, the braking capacity of shoe (A) is over twice that of shoe (B) for the same shoe size. Some manufacturers take advantage of this by making shoe (B) slightly smaller. This arrangement improves the design because the additional wheel surface exposure that isn't covered by an overly large shoe improves the heat dissipation capacity of the wheel.

The other major type of brake assembly is the disc brake (Fig. 7-4). Here the shoes pinch the rotating disc that is attached to the wheel, in much the same way you would use your fingers to pinch a coin. Disc brakes have no self-energizing features and are, therefore, frequently used with a power assist to boost the actuating force (F) to a de-

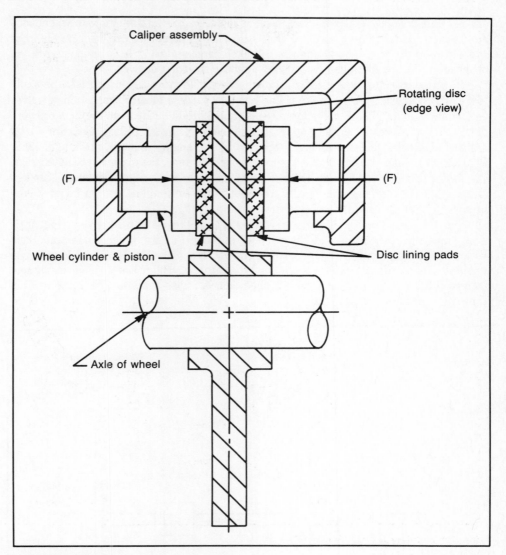

Fig. 7-4. Disc brake.

gree that proper braking can occur. Disc brakes are, however, self-adjusting. The brake lining pads retract enough to allow a slight drag. No adjustment is necessary, it is actually not even possible, on disc brakes.

As pointed out above, the rotating disc is a metal plate that is attached to and turns with the wheel. The caliper assembly straddles the rotating disc. This assembly is composed of brake cylinder (or cylinders), pistons, and disc shoe pads. As you apply the brake pedal, hydraulic pressure causes the wheel cylinder to expand the pistons, causing the disc shoe pads to press against both sides of the rotating disc.

Disc brakes are more exposed to cooling air than shoe brakes, so they dissipate heat faster and run cooler. This makes them less subject to swerving and fade than shoe brakes. The only problem with disc brakes is installation of a parking brake when discs are used on all four wheels. Because this is expensive, most cars use discs on the front and shoes on the rear. In addition, front brakes handle up to 75% of braking work, so installation of front discs and rear shoes is just plain good design.

Regardless of the type brakes used, the hydraulic system is practically the same (Fig. 7-5). It consists of the brake pedal, master cylinder, tubing, proportioning valve, and wheel cylinder. The braking force (F) is transmitted equally from the master cylinder to all four wheel cylinders by application of the brake pedal. If the brakes are power assisted, master cylinder pressure is boosted by the engine vacuum. Starting in 1968, all modern cars use a dual hydraulic system. In such systems, the master cylinder contains two fluid reservoirs, two pistons, and two brake lines: one line for the front wheel cylinders and one line for the rear wheel cylinders. Should one system fail, the car could still be brought to a stop using the other system.

The hydraulic fluid used in brake systems is a mineral oil with additives. Use super heavy-duty fluid for shoe brakes. It is amber in color. For disc brakes, use brake fluid with a high boiling point (500 degrees Fahrenheit). It is a blue-green color. You can use the disc brake fluid in a shoe-type system if the master cylinder has a rubber diaphragm underneath its cover, but never use a shoe fluid in a disc system. Check the level of the fluid at least twice per year.

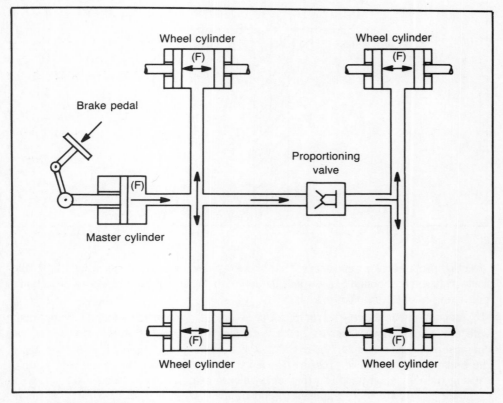

Fig. 7-5. Brake hydraulic system.

Wear

Each time the brakes are applied to slow down or stop the car, minute particles of friction material are worn away. Normally, this wear can proceed over 40,000 miles, until the lining material is so thin that replacement is necessary. This is considered normal. City or stop-and-go driving will wear linings much more quickly than long distance or highway driving.

Brakes work at their optimum when the frictional characteristics of the lining do not vary. To maintain the linings in this state is, of course, impossible. Actually, friction can vary with a number of conditions, including temperature, wear, and environment. Keep the linings dry and free of grease or brake fluid. If grease and brake fluid do build up, they cannot be cleaned from linings; replacement of the linings is necessary. Brakes that grab indicate a fluid-soaked lining.

Inspect the brake adjustment and lining thickness on shoe brakes twice a year. Brakes that drag too heavily on the wheel are a hazard and accelerated wear can be expected. If the brake drags too much it can become glazed or shiny. Glazed brakes tend to slip and are a safety hazard. Replacement might be required.

Perform a complete brake system inspection once a year. At this time, consider a thorough bleeding of all brake lines, cleaning of wheel assemblies, and honing of wheel cylinders. Keep the whole brake system in top shape for your personal safety and peace of mind. Refer to Table 7-2 for some representative brake system problems.

Table 7-2. Telltale Brake System Problems.

Symptom	Cause	Cure
Light brake pull when stopping	Front or rear brakes out of adjustment or worn	Adjust or replace
Strong brake pull when stopping	Front brake problem or faulty wheel alignment	Adjust or replace brake, align front end
Grinding or scraping noises when stopping	Worn brake linings	Replace linings
Clicking	Burred shoes	Replace shoes
Smell of brake fluid	Hydraulic system leak	Inspect and repair
Squeal	Caliper mounting bolts or adapter bracket loose	Adjust and tighten
Rattling or clanking on rough roads	Loose shoe and lining assembly	Adjust or replace
Pulsations in brake pedal	Wheel or disc untrue	Turn on lathe to true

*See any good auto service manual for many other symptoms, causes, and cures.

SUMMARY OF RECOMMENDATIONS

Shock Absorbers

- Always use heavy-duty shocks.
- Buy shocks that are lifetime guaranteed.
- Replace shocks about every 25,000 miles.
- Improve driving habits to increase shock life.

Exhaust System

- Combine a few short driving trips into one long one for better exhaust system part life.
- Buy mufflers and resonators that are lifetime guaranteed.
- Service the manifold heat control valve yearly.
- Inspect the exhaust system every time the car is on the lift or when rattles or hissing is heard underneath the car.

Brakes

- Use specified brake fluid only. Never mix fluids for use on shoe brakes with that for disc brakes.
- Check brake fluid level twice a year or when the pedal feels soft.
- Inspect the brake hydraulic system for leaks every time the car is on the lift.
- Consider metallic brake linings only for heavy trailoring use or when doing frequent mountain travel.
- Keep brake linings dry and free of grease and brake fluid.
- Adjust shoe-type brakes twice a year. Inspect for lining wear and thickness at the same interval.
- Perform a complete brake system check and cleaning once a year.

MECHANICS TIPS

Shock Absorbers

- Replace shock absorbers in pairs and all four at one time for best handling results.
- Don't buy bargain replacement shock absorbers; they won't last.
- Replacing shock absorbers can be a dirty and sometimes frustrating job. Leave it to your mechanic.

Exhaust System

- For emergency repairs, invest in a muffler repair kit and keep it handy, along with your other auto supplies.
- If you lose a muffler on the highway, don't panic. There is usually no safety concern, just a lot of noise. Get it replaced at your earliest convenience.
- Replacing mufflers and other exhaust system parts is a demanding, dirty job. Without a hydraulic lift the job can be a headache. Take the car to your mechanic or muffler specialty shop for best results.

Brakes

■ In wet weather, lightly apply the brakes periodically to keep them dry. This is especially important when driving through a lot of puddles.

■ Some brake materials have asbestos as part of the friction lining. When servicing the brakes, be careful not to breath in brake shoe lining dust or particles.

■ Your brakes are the major safety feature in your car. Keep them in perfect order.

8

Mechanical Tune-Ups

TUNE-UPS ARE JUST THE THING TO "PEP UP" ANY CAR, OLD OR RELATIVELY NEW. IN ORDER to get the best performance, mileage, and life from your car, you need to tune it twice a year. Tuning involves adjustment of worn parts or systems. There are many books published on this topic. In this chapter and the two following, we present theories and recommendations we hope will enable you to perform better, more complete tune-ups that will help prolong the life of your car. Again, follow the manufacturer's recommendations for performing the tune-ups themselves. Follow the recommendations given here for frequency of tune-ups and special tips. You'll be glad you did.

CARBURETION

An engine and a human being are alike at least in one respect; they both need fuel and air to function. In the case of our bodies, the fuel is the food we eat. In the car the fuel is either gasoline or diesel fuel. The carburetor, fuel pump, intake manifold, and valving all work together to provide the proper amounts of air and fuel to power the car.

The carburetor on your car is nothing more than a large air valve. When you depress the gas pedal you operate the carburetor by linkages or cables to allow more air to flow into the engine. The main job of the carburetor, then, is to introduce a proper air and fuel mixture into the engine cylinders under correct temperature and pressure.

Carburetor operation depends entirely upon differences in pressure within the carburetor. It works on the venturi principle (Fig. 8-1). Air flows through a tube, called a barrel, inside the carburetor. Most carburetors have one to four barrels, depending on engine size and the performance desired. As the air progresses downward toward

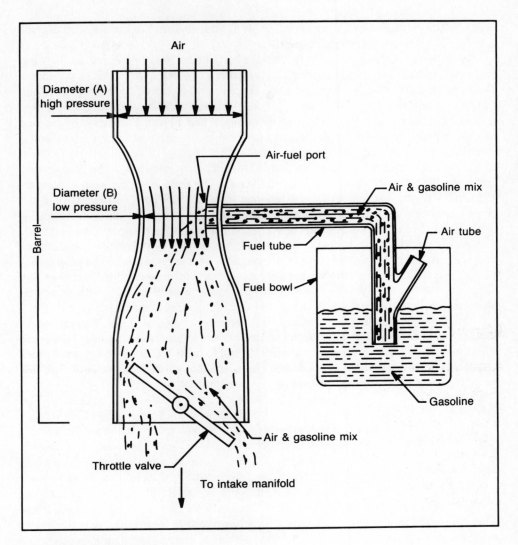

Fig. 8-1. Venturi principle.

the intake manifold, it encounters a necked-down or restricted area in the barrel. Since the diameter (B) in the figure is smaller than diameter (A), the air must speed up at the necked-down area in order to maintain the same amount of total air flow through the barrel: what goes in must come out.

As the air speeds up at the necked-down region of the barrel, its pressure drops, creating a partial vacuum. If we attach a fuel tube to the barrel in this region with the other end of the tube in a bucket (or bowl) of fuel, the fuel will be siphoned out of the bucket because of the vacuum effect. If we further attach an air tube to the fuel tube, as shown, air will be drawn into the fuel and a combination air-fuel mixture will flow into the barrel, through the intake manifold, and into the engine cylinders. A throttle valve located at the bottom of the barrel is connected via linkages or cables to the gas pedal to control the amount of air-fuel mixture delivered to the engine. The more air-fuel mixture delivered, the faster the engine speeds.

Modern carburetors are much more complicated than shown in Fig. 8-1. They are made up of numerous passages, ports, jets, and pumps to control not only the total amount of air-fuel mixture, but also the proportion of air to fuel delivered to the engine. When a higher proportion of gasoline to air is needed, the ratio is called a rich mix. Rich mixes are used at idle, for starting, and for accelerating. When a lower proportion of gasoline to air is needed, the ratio is called a lean mix. Lean mixes are used at any part-throttle operation.

Carburetors consist of a number of systems that do various jobs. The float system keeps gasoline at a constant level in the fuel bowl. The main metering system consists of tubing and jets that deliver the air-fuel mix from the fuel bowl to the barrel in the proper quantities. Each barrel has its own main metering system. The idle system supplies sufficient air-fuel mixture for engine operation at idle when the throttle valve is closed. The power/pump system is designed to supply the especially rich air-fuel mixture for the times that engine power and speed are required—for example, when passing another car. The choke system supplies the very rich air-fuel mixture needed for cold engine operation, as at start-up. The antistall dashpot system, used on cars with automatic transmission, acts to prevent stalling if the throttle is closed suddenly.

Our purpose here is not to explain carburetor operation in detail, but rather, to establish that, although the basic theory behind carburetor operation is simple, the many different driving conditions the car encounters tend to make the design complex. Proper engine performance and life depend on a clean, efficient carburetion system. For this reason, the carburetor must be kept in top condition.

Some high-performance cars use a fuel injection system instead of a carburetor. The air-fuel mixture is injected directly into each cylinder instead of being mixed before entry into the intake manifold, as with a carburetor. The advantage of a fuel injection system is that ideal fuel distribution is possible at every injection. This reduces fuel consumption and air pollution. The only disadvantages of a fuel injection system are the high cost and the fact that it must always be serviced by a factory-trained technician. In fact, work is often performed in a "clean room," which is not available to normal service stations. If your car has a fuel injection system, don't attempt your own service unless you know what you're doing. Have it checked out at least once a year for proper pressure levels, air-fuel mix, and performance. By the way, all diesel engines use fuel injection.

Now let's see how we can avoid problems and help lengthen the life of the carburetion system.

Air

Air is free. Gasoline costs money. Sometimes, we might forget that air (actually the oxygen in the air) is just as important to the operation of the engine as gasoline. The modern gasoline engine uses about 15 parts of air to 1 part of gasoline by weight. Gasoline weighs approximately 600 times as much as air at sea level. That means 1 pound of air will occupy 600 times as much space as 1 pound of gasoline. Therefore, we need to supply 600 × 15—or 9,000—cubic feet of air for every cubic foot of gasoline to run our cars. That's a lot of air to handle.

Air is supplied to the engine through an intake tube on the air cleaner assembly that is mounted on top of the carburetor. It must pass through a filter or air cleaner before it travels down through the carburetor barrel and into the engine. Atmospheric air contains dust and, especially in industrialized areas, may carry particles of dirt, smoke, and coal—which are abrasive. In heavy traffic, the air will be contaminated with car exhaust, which can contain droplets of unburned or partially burned gasoline or oil. The air cleaner must filter all these pollutants and abrasives out of the air before they reach the carburetor.

There are two types of air filters in common passenger car use: the dry corrugated paper filter and the oil bath filter. In either filter type, the filtering medium must not be torn, clogged, or overly dirty. Inspect the filters every other month.

With the dry paper filter, hold the filter up to a bright light. You should be able to see light through the corrugations. If not, try to tap the filter or blow air from inside out to clean it, otherwise replace it. For optimum performance and cleanliness, replace the air filter once per year regardless, because many times small holes that allow dirt to pass into the engine go unnoticed even though the filter looks clean.

Oil bath filters need to be cleaned every six months or sooner, as conditions warrant. Clean with the specified solvent and reassemble according to manufacturer's instructions.

With either type filter, be sure the elements are properly seated atop the carburetor to prevent unfiltered air leakage in the carburetor. Remember: dirt is the biggest enemy of your car engine.

Fuel

Petroleum is the second most plentiful liquid on earth. Only water is more plentiful. Crude petroleum oil is a mix of many different kinds of hydrocarbons. Gasoline, diesel fuel, jet fuel, lubricating oil, kerosene, grease, plastics, and many other products originate from crude petroleum oil. All gasolines are hydrocarbons. The complete combustion of any hydrocarbon with pure oxygen yields water, carbon dioxide, and energy. Because air contains other gases besides oxygen, many other combustion products are realized. Pollution control equipment on modern cars is designed to neutralize or render harmless otherwise environmentally harmful combustion products.

The chemistry of gasoline is a complex subject. Gasoline formulations include additives to act as varnish removers and cleaners, additives to improve burnability, additives to increase octane number and, for cold weather driving, additives to rid the gasoline of water vapor. As a car owner, there are some additives you can add to your fuel tank. They include cleaning solvents and water vapor absorbers (made basically of alcohol).

All major name-brand gasolines are suitable for use in a modern car engine. The only areas in which you need to make a choice are in octane numbers. Scientifically, the octane number of gasoline is the percentage by volume of iso-octane (2, 2, 4 trimethylpentane) in a mixture of iso-octane and normal heptane. Iso-octane is the substance needed to prevent knocking. The more iso-octane a particular gasoline has, the higher the octane number. Normally, the higher the octane number of a particular gasoline, the less it will knock, and the more power, better performance, and better mileage you will get. If a particular fuel performs better than pure iso-octane, its octane number can be greater than 100. Aviation fuels are typically rated at 130 and above.

At the fuel pump you might notice a label stating that octane numbers are arrived at using the (R & M)/2 method. The R stands for the Research Octane Number (RON), the M stands for the Motor Octane Number (MON). The RON is a measure of antiknock performance under mild operating conditions at low to medium engine speeds. The MON

Table 8-1. Antiknock Requirements for Gasoline.

Octane Number	Application
(RON + MON)/2	
Less than 87 87	For cars with low antiknock needs. For most 1971 and later cars.
89	For most 1970 and prior cars designed to operate on regular gasoline.
92	For some cars designed to run on premium gasolines.
95 – 97.5	For most 1970 and prior cars with high compression ratio engines, and for later model cars with high compression ratio engines.

Note: The octane number for use in areas where altitude is greater than 2,000 feet may be reduced 0.5 number for each succeeding 500 feet, but is not to exceed a total of three octane numbers.

is a measure of antiknock performance under severe conditions during power acceleration at high speeds. Averaging these two numbers gives an indication of overall performance of the particular gasoline. Table 8-1 lists current antiknock requirements for gasolines.

Check with the owner's manual, dealer, or manufacturer in regard to the minimum octane number gasoline for use in your car. Ask about using higher octane number gasolines and any associated changes in engine timing or carburetor adjustment. If permitted by the manufacturer, always use a gasoline of the highest octane number. In other words, always use the hi-test gasoline. Your engine will run smoother, you'll feel more power at the pedal, and your car will get better gas mileage. In addition, many of the hi-test gasolines have additional cleaners incorporated into their chemistry, so in time your car will run cleaner also.

Caution: Never use a leaded gasoline in an engine designed to run on unleaded gasoline or vice versa. Stick with the factory recommended type only. And stay away from gasolines formulated with alcohol; their use may void car warranties.

Other than using the best gasoline available, proper filtering is really the only concern in regard to fuel. Inspect the gasoline filters on the car twice a year. Replace them if they are dirty or clogged. Consider replacement once a year regardless, because the replacement cost is so low.

Ignition

The ignition is affected by the mechanical timing adjustment. Adjust the timing to specification twice per year. Timing out of adjustment leads to poor performance and wasted fuel. Ignition will be covered more fully in Chapter 9.

Problems

Some problems with the air-fuel delivery system include ping, knock, and rough idle.

Ping. Ping is actually a light knock that results from post-ignition. Post-ignition occurs when some unburned fuel ignites spontaneously after the spark plug has fired the major portion of fuel. This creates two pressure fronts that collide like a thunderstorm inside the cylinder, creating very high pressures and temperatures. Normally, a slight ping while accelerating or driving up a hill is not cause for concern. However, it does indicate that something is wrong and, if left uncorrected, could cause problems.

Ping can result from using gasoline with too low an octane rating, incorrect ignition timing, overheating engine, and incorrect spark plugs, to name just a few. Correct ping as soon as practical.

Knock. Knock is a more serious form of engine ping. It basically is abnormal combustion, occurring before the spark plug fires or at pre-ignition. It can become so severe that it causes piston rings to break and can even burn holes through piston heads. It is usually caused by hot carbon deposits inside the cylinder or on the piston, high valve temperatures, or incorrect spark plugs. Knock must be corrected immediately. It can lead to diminished engine life and/or complete engine failure.

BOLTING

Don't overlook bolting when performing a tune-up. Loose bolting can lead to performance-robbing air leaks, unnecessary vibration of engine parts, and in some cases, loss of engine parts simply because they fall off the car.

Before you start your actual tune-up, take a trip around the engine compartment and check for any loose bolting. Tighten engine bolting to specification twice a year. In particular, check for loose carburetor to intake manifold bolting, air cleaner assembly to carburetor bolting, intake and exhaust manifold to engine bolting, head to block bolting, oil cover bolting, battery case bolting, and bolting that secures any and all auxiliary equipment to the engine proper or fender or fire wall.

Do not overtighten any bolting. Tighten only to specification and in the factory-specified sequence, if any. Be especially careful not to overtighten the air cleaner assembly to the carburetor. This bolting can easily be stripped or pulled out of the carburetor body.

COMPRESSION AND VACUUM

Compression and vacuum are the two keys to proper engine breathing. Compression and vacuum adjusted to factory-designed levels allow the engine to develop full power and efficiency. Let's discuss compression first.

All modern gasoline-powered passenger car engines base their operation on the four-stroke cycle. These strokes, in order of occurrence, are: intake, compression, power, and exhaust.

The intake stroke starts as the piston moves down through the cylinder from the uppermost (top) position in the cylinder. As the piston moves downward, it creates a partial vacuum, which helps to draw the air-fuel mixture into the cylinder through the intake valve.

The compression stroke begins as the piston reverses direction at the end of the intake stroke to start moving upward within the cylinder. With both the intake and exhaust valves closed, the air-fuel mixture has no place to go, so it becomes compressed. As the piston continues its upward movement, it compresses the air-fuel mixture more and more, raising its pressure to a limit as designed at the factory.

The power stroke begins as the piston nears the top of the cylinder at completion of the compression stroke. Just before the piston reaches its uppermost travel in the cylinder, the spark plug fires, igniting the compressed air-fuel mixture. The subsequent explosion expands the burning fuel mixture and drives the piston downward, and because it is attached to the crankshaft, helps turn the engine and move the car.

The exhaust stroke finishes the cycle as the piston again reverses direction to start another upward trip through the cylinder. During this time the exhaust valve opens, allowing the piston to push the burned gases out of the cylinder and into the exhaust system.

The importance of the compression stroke on engine power levels and efficiency is paramount. For the engine to meet its full power capability, the degree of compression measured in pounds per square inch (psi) must meet design specifications. It's also important that compression readings for all cylinders be compared with the maximum variation between cylinders as specified by the factory. Checking compression is the only way to make sure that the pistons, piston rings, valves, and cylinder head gasket are properly sealing. You cannot perform a proper tune-up until compression problems are solved. Here are a few things to consider.

Let's establish the specified compression pressure for your imaginary V-8 engine at 130 to 160 psi with a maximum variation between cylinders of 25 psi, for example. The first set of readings shown would indicate that the engine is breathing well.

Cylinder		
	# 1—140 psi	# 5—140 psi
	# 2—135 psi	# 6—140 psi
	# 3—135 psi	# 7—145 psi
	# 4—140 psi	# 8—135 psi

All the cylinders are within both specified factory limits.

The next set of readings indicate a problem with cylinder #3. It is not below specified pressure, but it is below the maximum variation of pressure as compared to cylinder #4. (160 psi − 130 psi = 30 psi).

Cylinder		
	# 1—160 psi	# 5—160 psi
	# 2—155 psi	# 6—160 psi
	# 3—130 psi	# 7—155 psi
	# 4—160 psi	# 8—155 psi

A third example shows that a couple of cylinders, #2 and #6, are below the minimum specified pressure—indicating a worn engine.

Cylinder		
	# 1—135 psi	# 5—130 psi
	# 2—120 psi	# 6—125 psi
	# 3—135 psi	# 7—130 psi
	# 4—130 psi	# 8—130 psi

Low compression pressure in cylinders that are adjacent to one another may indicate piston ring leakage and/or valve leakage. Low-pressure readings in adjacent cylinders can be a sign of cylinder head gasket leakage. Higher-than-specified readings are harmful to the engine, also. They indicate carbon build-up in the cylinders. Any of these problems must be corrected as soon as possible.

As pointed out earlier, changing the engine oil, the oil filter, the air filter, gas filters, and maintaining proper bolting torque on engine parts will help to keep abrasive dirt out of the cylinder area. Dirt can cause cylinder, piston ring, and valve wear that eventually lead to low compression pressure readings. To further guard against cylinder compression pressure problems, consider using any of the quality cylinder head cleaners or top oils available on the market. They remove potentially harmful carbon and varnish deposits. They usually work by either adding them to the gas tank or directly through the carburetor. Follow directions on the can. Perform this preventive maintenance procedure once a year.

The other way the engine breathes is through intake manifold vacuum. Intake manifold vacuum is the decrease in air pressure created by the pistons moving downward within the cylinders. Intake manifold vacuum helps to operate the heater controls, power brakes, distributor advance mechanism, antipollution controls, automatic transmission modulator and, in some vehicles, the windshield wipers. The amount of vacuum depends upon engine speed and load. It is also affected by the condition of the pistons, piston rings, valves, exhaust system, and by proper engine bolt torque. While vacuum readings that are slightly out of factory specification do not need to be cause for alarm, they should be corrected because poor vacuum will affect engine performance. Table 8-2 explains how to interpret vacuum gauge readings.

To keep manifold vacuum up to par, repair any of the problems indicated in Table 8-2 as soon as possible. Check for leaks between the intake manifold and engine block, the intake manifold and carburetor mounting, and at hoses and other vacuum lines throughout the engine. Other than fixing leaks, keeping the cylinders, pistons, and valves clean by using the cleaners or top oils discussed under engine compression pressure

Table 8-2. Interpreting Vacuum Gauge Readings.

Reading	Cause
Vacuum pointer drops	Sticking valves due to gum or varnish deposits, carbon buildup, weak valve springs, bent valve stems, sticking valve lifters.
Pointer floats up and down	Incorrect air-fuel mixture.
Low vacuum reading	Leaks, compression problems, late ignition, valve timing out of adjustment.
Unsteady readings	Leaks, carburetor adjustment needed, incorrect distributor point spacing, valve adjustment needed.
Slowing dropping readings	Restricted exhaust system—probably plugged muffler or catalytic converter.

is the only preventive maintenance you can perform for the metal parts of the vacuum system. For rubber vacuum hoses, consider replacing them every 25,000 miles or two years, or when they develop leaks through cracking.

FUEL PUMP

Car designers need to provide a means to supply the carburetor with a sufficient quantity of gasoline at the correct pressure to meet a variety of driving conditions. In very old cars, this was typically accomplished by mounting the gas tank somewhere above the carburetor, which allowed the gasoline to simply spill into the carburetor. Modern high-performance engines need to have the gasoline properly pressurized, therefore, the older gravity method of fuel supply would not work.

Fuel pumps move the gasoline from the fuel tank under pressure and supply it to the carburetor in precisely the correct amount at the needed time. Fuel pumps are either mechanical and run directly off a cam inside the engine, or are electrical and run from electrical power supplied by the car's electrical system. One advantage of an electric fuel pump is that it can be located away from the hot engine, thus reducing the chance of vapor lock in the pump. In either case, the fuel pump acts to keep the carburetor fuel bowl filled with gasoline.

Fuel pumps are notoriously long-lasting, usually requiring little service. However, when their performance drops off or they begin to fail, they should be repaired or replaced immediately. For example, a ruptured diaphragm in a mechanical fuel pump will result in a leak between the engine crankcase and intake manifold. This will cause engine oil to be drawn into the cylinders, fouling the carburetor, spark plugs, valves, and cylinders. Antipollution equipment can also be fouled via this failure.

Modern fuel pumps normally cannot be repaired; they must be replaced. There is no service you can perform on most of them. Some pumps, especially on older cars, can be repaired or rebuilt. Rebuilding kits are available for this. If your car has a mechanical fuel pump, consider replacing or rebuilding every 100,000 miles. Electric fuel pumps can be run until they develop problems. Fuel pumps for diesel-powered cars are susceptible to water damage. Use a dry gas formulated to be added to diesel fuel to absorb water in the fuel tank. For best results, add every 12,000 miles.

Test fuel pump operation for specified pressure flow and vacuum every year or 12,000 miles. An avid practitioner of car care will also consider having the gas tank cleaned and flushed every 2 years or 25,000 miles to keep abrasive dust and dirt away from the fuel pump.

VALVES

There are three types of valves on modern cars you should be aware of: engine valves, exhaust gas recirculation valves, and positive crankcase ventilation valves.

Engine Valves

Every cylinder in the car has two valves. The intake valve allows the air-fuel mixture to flow into the cylinder at the proper time during the intake stroke. The exhaust valve allows burned fuel to exit the cylinder at the proper time during the exhaust stroke.

During the compression and power strokes, the valves must remain tightly sealed. To do this, valves are precision-ground along their edges to seal against the cylinder valve seat, which is also precision-ground. Carbon buildup, or varnish and other foreign particles such as abrasive dirt, will foul or scratch these smoothly ground surfaces and impair valve sealing—and, therefore, engine performance. Valve grinding is necessary from time to time to keep these surfaces in top condition. Have the valves ground every 100,000 miles, assuming no problems develop before then.

Valves need to be kept in perfect alignment to facilitate good sealing as the valve closes on the valve seat. Valve guides provide this alignment. The valve stem moves

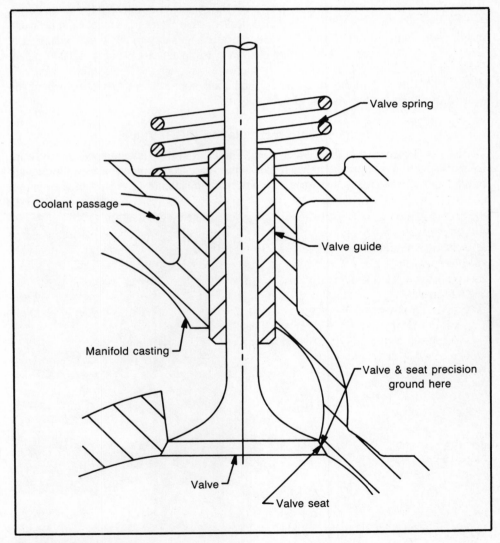

Fig. 8-2. Valve assembly.

up and down through the valve guide in a precision fit that does not allow any appreciable side play (Fig. 8-2). If the valve guides are the replaceable type, install new ones or have them reamed every time the valves are ground.

The valve spring is the other major component of the engine valve assembly. It provides the correct force against which valves open and close. A weak spring will cause improper valve seating, resulting in poor engine performance and possible damage to the valve. A spring that is too strong or distorted could result in excessive camshaft lobe wear. Test the springs every 100,000 miles at valve regrinding time.

Valves are operated by rocker arms, actuated by push rods and lifters on non-overhead cam engines. As the camshaft rotates, it operates the lifter which, in turn, moves the pushrod. The pushrod acts to pivot the rocker arm, pushing the valve down. For proper valve closure, a slight clearance—called valve clearance—must exist between the closed valve and rocker arm. This clearance is necessary to allow for expansion of warm engine valve parts. Adjust this clearance to specification every 12,000 miles. Overhead camshaft engines might or might not require periodic valve clearance adjustment. Check with the shop manual, and if adjustment is required, perform at the same interval as for non-overhead cam engines.

Exhaust Gas Recirculation (EGR) Valve

The EGR valve is a part of the EGR System. The EGR system is an antipollution system. It diverts some of the engine exhaust gases into the cylinder, which acts to lower high combustion temperatures that form nitrogen oxide pollutants. The part of the system

Fig. 8-3. EGR valve.

that diverts this flow is the EGR valve. Because cold engines produce no nitrogen oxide, the EGR valve operates only in warm and hot engines. The EGR valve is normally operated by engine vacuum and mounted on the intake manifold near the carburetor (Fig. 8-3).

Pinging, rough idle, and excessive production of nitrogen oxide as revealed by an emission test are telltale signs of problems with the EGR valve. Check vacuum hoses periodically for leakage or blockage and proper attachment to the EGR valve. A sticking EGR valve can sometimes free up if carbon deposits are cleaned from the valve stem and port area. Clean the EGR valve twice a year. If cleaning doesn't free the valve, it must be replaced.

Positive Crankcase Ventilation (PCV) Valve

The job of the PCV valve is to return combustion gases to the carburetor that have leaked or blown past the piston rings and collected in the crankcase. Years ago these gases were merely ventilated to the atmosphere. Now, with strict air pollution control requirements, we can't get away with simple venting to outside air (Fig. 8-4).

On modern cars, a vacuum hose runs from the rocker arm cover to the base of the carburetor. Engine vacuum draws combustion vapors from the crankcase, into the rocker arm area, and out into the intake manifold, where they are mixed with fresh air-fuel mixture for burning. The PCV valve regulates this flow of vapor.

Over time, the PCV valve will clog from an accumulation of sludge carried with the crankcase vapors. When the PCV clogs it will no longer be able to pull pollutants from the crankcase, and acids, sludge, and engine oil will build up and foul the engine.

Check the PCV system every 5,000 miles. Perform tests according to factory recommendations. Completely clean the system once a year or every 12,000 miles. Make sure all hoses are in good shape. If the PCV valve on your car is the cleanable type,

Fig. 8-4. PCV valve.

69

clean it every 12,000 miles with the recommended solvent—otherwise replace it every 12,000 miles.

SUMMARY OF RECOMMENDATIONS

- Perform a mechanical tune-up twice a year.
- Keep carburetor linkages clean and lubed.
- If your car has fuel injection, have the system checked yearly.
- Inspect air filters every other month. Replace the dry paper type once a year. Clean the oil bath types twice a year.
- Use the highest octane number gasoline you can get.
- Inspect fuel filters twice a year. Replace yearly.
- Tighten to specification all engine bolting twice a year.
- Use cylinder cleaners or top oil once a year.
- Replace rubber vacuum hoses at 25,000 miles, or every two years or when cracked or hardened.
- Test fuel pump operation every 12,000 miles or yearly. Consider replacing or rebuilding mechanical fuel pumps every 100,000 miles, or sooner if trouble develops.
- Dress valves every 100,000 miles. Install new or ream old valve guides at this time. Also, test valve springs at 100,000 miles.
- Adjust valve clearance on those cars that can be adjusted every 12,000 miles.
- Clean the EGR valve every 6 months.
- Check the PCV system every 5,000 miles. Clean the system every 12,000 miles. Replace PCV valves that can't be cleaned every 12,000 miles.

MECHANIC'S TIPS

- Keep a supply of mechanical tune-up parts available with your other auto supplies for both routine and emergency service.
- Don't try to service fuel injection systems yourself. They require almost "clean room" service. Even small amounts of dirt can impair their performance.
- Buy the better grades of air and fuel filters. They are more efficient and protect your engine better.
- Keep gasoline, oil, and solvents off rubber hosing.
- Learn to wipe down the engine and related mechanical equipment every few months. This little task will help to get dirt out of places where it can do harm.
- When servicing the carburetor air filter, keep the throat of the carburetor covered with a clean, lint-free rag, a piece of plastic, or aluminum foil to keep dirt out of the carburetor.
- Vacuum the carburetor air filter holder twice a year.

9

Electrical Tune-Ups

THE ELECTRICAL SYSTEM IN YOUR CAR ACTS, IN A SENSE, LIKE THE NERVOUS SYSTEM IN your body. It provides control over various engine parts; supplies power to run and activate numerous devices and systems; and raises alarm through sensors, warning lights, and buzzers. The complete system is composed of a starter circuit, an ignition circuit, a charging circuit, and various lighting circuits and accessory circuits. We will deal only with those elements of the electrical system that normally require periodic maintenance.

THE CAR BATTERY

The battery is the heart of the electrical system. With the engine off, the battery supplies current to operate the lights and accessories. It supplies the power to start the engine via the starter and ignition systems. The car battery is actually a miniature power plant that stores energy in chemical form (Fig. 9-1).

There are two main types of batteries for passenger car use: the lead-acid battery and the alkaline battery. The lead-acid type is used in the vast majority of cars and is the one referred to in this text. Because most modern automotive electrical systems are rated at 12 volts, we will concentrate only on 12-volt systems.

The modern 12-volt, lead-acid storage battery is made up of 6 cells, each able to supply approximately 2 volts. They are electrically connected inside the battery case to supply the needed 12 volts. Each cell is constructed of two sets of plates immersed in an electrolyte, which is composed of sulfuric acid and water. Normally, one set of plates is made from porous lead while the other is made from lead peroxide.

The cells work on the principle of ion transfer. The electrolyte reacts chemically with the plates, resulting in an accumulation of positive ions on the lead peroxide plate.

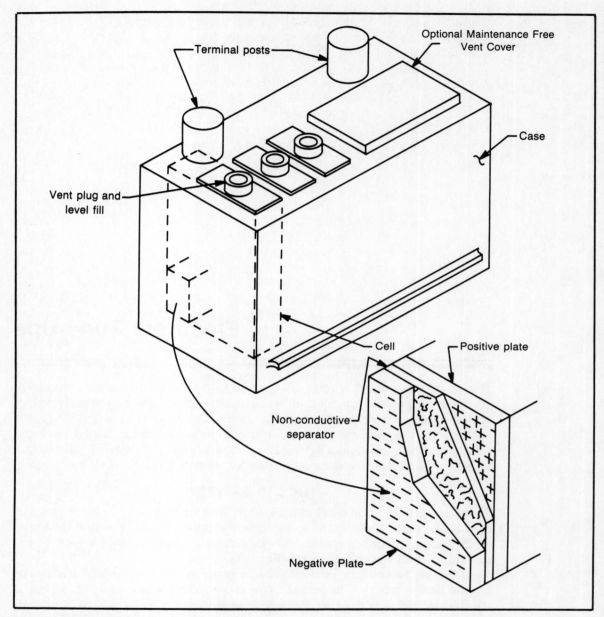

Fig. 9-1. Typical car battery.

This gives it a positive charge. As the positive ions leave the lead plate, it becomes more and more negatively charged. Electric current then flows from plate to plate and is added up from all the battery cells to flow from one battery terminal through the electrical system, back to the other battery terminal and into the electrolyte again.

As the battery is continually called upon to supply electricity, the chemical reaction within the cells forms a coating of lead sulfate on the surface of the plates. The battery becomes weaker as this coating builds up. It eventually goes dead when the plates have been coated with sulfate, to the point where an electrical charge cannot go through the thick sulfate coating.

Batteries are rated in a number of ways. Cold-start capacity is probably the most important. Cold-start capacity is the number of amperes a battery can deliver to the starting circuit at 0 degrees Fahrenheit for 30 seconds before cell voltage falls below 1.2 volts. A cold engine can draw as much as 400 amps from the battery during starting. This is extremely high current draw. Never crank the engine on cold start for more than 30 seconds at a time to help avoid premature battery discharge.

Wear

Normal battery wear is caused by sulfation of the cell plates, as explained above. Recharging will usually reverse the sulfation process and restore the cell plates to their original condition. It is advisable to recharge the battery as it weakens, rather than when it is completely dead. Some battery cell plates can become so encrusted with sulfate that they may disintegrate or cause short circuits within the cell.

In normal battery operation, gases are given off that can promote terminal corrosion. Terminal corrosion will reduce current flow through the battery cables and on into the electrical system. Check for terminal corrosion twice a year and clean as required. Coat the terminals with petroleum jelly or a special terminal coating made of white grease to help prevent future corrosion. Making sure the cable ends fit tightly around the terminals also helps reduce corrosion.

Batteries can also become drained or fail prematurely from other causes. If the battery periodically requires a considerable amount of water, it is being overcharged. Overcharging will eventually cause the cell plates to buckle and fail. Check out the charging system and bring it to factory specifications.

A cracked battery case can be caused by hold-down clamps that are either too tight or too loose. A bulged case can be caused by a hold-down clamp that's too tight.

Additional corrosion can be caused by a dirty battery top. A dirty battery top collects salts that provide an electrical path from terminal to terminal on batteries. This causes loss of battery power and further corrosion. Clean battery cases once a year, or as needed, to avoid this.

Care

Batteries are husky and heavy, and if properly mounted, need very little periodic care. Provide the care mentioned above to correct and prevent problems.

Check the water level in the battery every month and bring to the fill line. Maintenance-free or low-maintenance batteries can be checked less often. Check the battery charge with a hydrometer. The hydrometer measures the density of the electrolyte in each cell. Fully charged batteries show hydrometer readings of 1.265 or more. A fully discharged battery will test at about 1.150. Follow the directions that come with the hydrometer to properly perform the test and interpret the readings.

When filling the battery with water, there is no need to use distilled water. Most battery manufacturers fill batteries with drinking water. Use distilled or bottled water only if your water supply is hard and/or has iron-bearing minerals or iron bacteria dissolved in it. Never add acid to the battery. Acid doesn't evaporate and, in a sense, is never used up. And never put any kind of battery additives into the battery. Although these are supposed to enhance ion transfer in older batteries, their effectiveness is still questionable. By the way, if you pour a battery additive into the battery, you will void your battery warranty.

Keep the battery charged to at least 75% charge at all times. A hydrometer reading of about 1.230 indicates a 75% charge. Recharge the battery when readings fall below 1.230. In the winter you may want to supply a trickle charge overnight for continued ease of starting in very cold weather. Trickle charging should not be used extensively, however, because it can cause overcharging of the battery.

For extremely cold weather consider using a battery or engine warmer when starting the car. Battery warmers run on house current and either wrap around the battery like a blanket or are a pad type on which the battery sits. A warm battery will provide better starting on cold mornings.

Also, for cold-weather starting, consider one of a number of engine heaters on the market. The in-line type heater pushes warmed engine coolant through the engine block. It is spliced into the heater outlet hose. The block type heater is mounted in place of a core plug in the engine block. It has an electric heating element that directly heats engine coolant in the water jacket. The radiator hose heater type is spliced into the lower radiator hose. It also heats engine coolant. Tank heaters are mounted between the heater outlet hose and the drain opening on the engine block. Lastly, there is the dipstick heater that merely slides into the oil dipstick tube and warms the oil. It is the least expensive and simplest heating device to install.

ELECTRICAL CONNECTIONS AND WIRING

The cause of many mysterious problems is often no more than loose, dirty, damaged or corroded electrical connections. It is important to clean and tighten all loose electrical connections. Loose connections may cause arcing between a terminal and wire connector. Loose connections also allow dirt and grime to collect at the terminations, leading to poor conduction of electricity. Check, clean, and tighten all electrical connections before performing any tune-up work and at least twice per year.

Check for cracked, torn, or blistered insulation on wiring. Blistering might be caused by excessive heat. Make sure wires are routed correctly in the engine compartment, especially any wiring that is blistered. Replace defective or worn wiring with the factory-recommended type.

Checking the ignition (spark) wiring is important. Cracks in the insulation can lead to high-voltage leaks and engine misfire. Ignition cables should not be cracked, burned, (too close to manifolding) or brittle. Ignition cables are available with three types of insulation: silicone, hypalon, and neoprene.

Silicone is used on modern cars with pollution-control equipment. These cars tend to run hot and need the greater heat resistance in cabling offered with silicone insulation. Hypalon and neoprene are all right for use in older cars, they will not last nearly as long as silicone. At replacement time, consider using ignition cables with silicone insulation.

Another choice you need to make when replacing ignition cables is the type of conductor you desire. Carbon-impregnated fabric cables are easily damaged and very fragile. They can't be bent or abused. Use ignition cables with conductors made from aramid fibers or shielded metal wire. They are much stronger than the cables with carbon-impregnated fabric conductors.

Test ignition cables with an ohmmeter twice a year. Refer to the shop manual for the correct procedure to use and the readings you should expect. Replace defective wiring as required.

SPARK PLUGS

After the air-fuel mixture is delivered to the cylinder and sufficiently compressed during the compression stroke, it is ignited by a high-voltage spark generated between the electrodes of the spark plug. To produce the desired combustion of the air-fuel mixture, the spark must be at a high energy level during all engine speeds. Maintaining the spark plug is the easiest, and probably one of the most important, things you can do to maintain good gas mileage and engine efficiency.

The spark plug is nothing more than a center metal electrode that is surrounded by a ceramic insulator. The bottom of the ceramic insulator is fitted into a metal threaded casing that screws into the cylinder head. This casing contains the hex that fits into the spark plug socket wrench. Another electrode is welded to this metal casing. The electrode on the metal casing and the center electrode are separated by a small air gap through which the spark must jump.

It takes a certain amount of high-voltage energy for the spark to jump the air gap between the electrodes. If the gap is too large, the spark will not have enough energy to jump across, and engine misfiring will occur. If the gap is too small, the spark may not be of sufficient energy to ignite the air-fuel mixture, and poor gas mileage and fouled plugs could result. Check and adjust the spark plug gap twice per year and at every tune-up. Remember, one spark plug that misfires can increase gasoline consumption as much as 35% in a four-cylinder engine and up to 15% in a V-8 engine.

At replacement time, buy only new (not reconditioned), brand name spark plugs. Some stores offer them on sale from time to time. Stock up on them; their cost is minimal. Consider replacing plugs every 15,000 miles. In addition to choosing a brand name, you must also choose the heat range of the plug.

Plugs for most cars come in a variety of heat ranges. The heat range is a measure of the plug's ability to transfer heat from the insulator end near the gap area to the engine block. A so-called hot plug transfers heat slowly, staying hot. A cold plug will transfer heat more quickly and run cooler. Be sure you are using the correct heat range for your type of driving. If the plug is too hot, it will ignite the air-fuel mixture before it sparks, causing pinging. If the plug is too cold, it will not burn away combustion deposits in the gap area and may cause fouling. Use hot plugs for mostly city or stop-and-go driving. For highway or long-distance driving, use a cooler plug. The normal plug that is recommended for the car is intended for a mixture of highway and stop-and-go driving.

Normal Wear

Normal spark plug wear is caused by the interaction of the high-energy spark and the corrosive combustion gases that gradually attack and disintegrate the electrodes. The gap will slowly widen, resulting in decreased ignition efficiency. If the electrodes have not been worn down too much, a simple cleaning and regapping will bring the plugs back

Fig. 9-2. Normal spark plug wear (Courtesy of Champion Spark Plug Company).

to design performance level. Although plugs can last up to 30,000 miles, we don't advise cleaning and regapping past 15,000 to 20,000 miles. Considering their cost, it's better to just replace them. Worn plugs that are regapped can still cause loss of engine power and speed, decreased gas mileage, and hard starting (Fig. 9-2).

Abnormal Wear

Premature plug wear or failure is usually a sign of problems with the ignition system or the engine.

Black, wet deposits (Fig. 9-3) are normally caused by oil leaking past worn piston rings or valve guides. In rare cases, these wet deposits can result from leakage of brake fluid past the brake booster diaphragm or automatic transmission fluid leaking past the automatic transmission modulator.

Black, dry deposits (Fig. 9-4) can be caused by too rich an air-fuel mixture, weak ignition sparking, or use of plugs with a heat range that is too cold.

Red, dry deposits are harmless, but should be cleaned from the plug. They are caused by manganese antiknock additives in unleaded gasoline.

A sign of an overheating plug is dark brown spots on the bottom of the insulator (Fig. 9-5). If the car is not pinging and the air-fuel mixture is not too lean, then suspect that the plug is being used at too high a heat range. Switching to a colder plug may help. If overheating is not corrected, the electrodes will quickly erode and the insulator may blister (Fig. 9-6). Also, check for a leak in the intake manifold near the affected cylinder.

Most modern cars use unleaded gasoline. For those engines that still run on leaded gas, the deposits shown in Fig. 9-7 are indicative of lead fouling. These deposits are usually brown to light yellow or even white in color. If the electrodes are still in good shape, cleaning will bring the plug up to snuff.

Fig. 9-3. Oil-fouled spark plug (Courtesy of Champion Spark Plug Company).

77

Fig. 9-4. Spark plug showing incorrect air-fuel mixture (Courtesy of Champion Spark Plug Company).

Learn to look for and recognize patterns of plug wear or failure as well. Fouling of rear plugs might only indicate that the oil drain holes in the back of the cylinder head of V-8 engines are clogged or restricted. Overheating of rear plugs might also point to cooling system blockage in the water jacket. Two adjacent center plugs that are fouled on four- or six-cylinder engines could indicate a too-rich air-fuel mixture in the carburetor. In addition, two adjacent plugs fouled in a four- or six-cylinder engine or in one bank of a V-8 engine might be caused by a blown head gasket. These are the kinds of things a good mechanic would look for.

DISTRIBUTOR, ALTERNATOR, AND TIMING

The distributor and alternator are part of the ignition system. The timing is the setting or adjustment of the distributor that allows smooth, sequential firing of the engine spark plugs. The distributor and alternator are the two components of the ignition system that normally require periodic maintenance, and so are covered here in some detail.

The combination of distributor and coil receives the low-voltage electricity from the alternator and steps it up to the high voltage needed to jump the spark plug gap. This

Fig. 9-5. Overheated spark plug (Courtesy of Champion Spark Plug Company).

Fig. 9-6. Spark plug with blistered insulator (Courtesy of Champion Spark Plug Company).

Fig. 9-7. Additive-fouled spark plug (Courtesy of Champion Spark Plug Company).

higher voltage may approach 50,000 volts. Figure 9-8 is a simplified schematic of a typical breaker point ignition system, showing the alternator, ignition switch, coil, and distributor.

Most modern cars manufactured since 1974 have electronic ignition systems. However, older American cars and a few modern imported ones use the breaker point system. Breaker points are located inside the distributor assembly. They are mechanical contact points that act as a switch to periodically turn on and off the low-voltage current flowing through the primary winding of the coil. This low-voltage current induces a sufficient high-voltage current in the secondary winding of the coil which, in turn, is distributed via the rotor and distributor cap in a timed sequence (correct firing order) to the spark plugs.

The rotor is driven by the distributor shaft, which is geared to the engine camshaft in such a manner that the rotor will turn at half the crankshaft speed. This arrangement allows delivery of a spark to each cylinder once during every four-stroke cycle of the engine.

There are a number of moving parts in the breaker point distributor and, of course, moving parts eventually wear or need adjustment. The breaker points commonly require

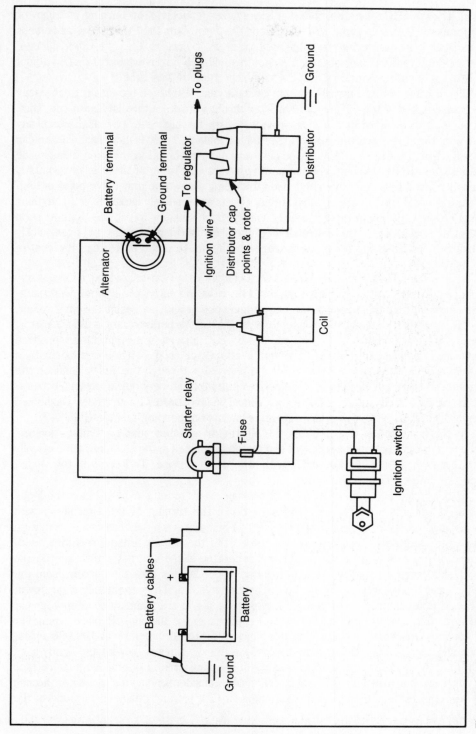

Fig. 9-8. Breaker point ignition.

the most care. Examine the points twice a year, checking for burning, pitting, or misalignment. Be sure to lubricate the cam on the distributor shaft that opens and closes the breaker points with the recommended grease. Be sure to lubricate other parts of the distributor also, as indicated in the shop manual. Do not overlubricate. Also adjust the breaker point gap and dwell angle to specification at this time.

Check and clean the distributor cap twice a year. High-voltage current can easily leak from cracked or frayed ignition cables, or through cracks in the distributor cap. Dirt, grease, or carbon buildup can also provide a path for high-energy leaks. Clean any corrosion from the cap terminals with a brush or replace, if necessary. Replace the cap or rotor if either is cracked. Also, if the electrical contacts on the rotor or on those inside the cap are pitted or burned, replacement is indicated. Pitting of the breaker points is normally caused by a defective condenser. Installing a new one may solve point pitting.

As a general rule, breaker point distributor parts are relatively inexpensive. If anything seems wrong with any of the parts, it is usually much cheaper to replace them as soon as possible rather than to try to stretch their useful life. Worn distributor parts can quickly cost dollars in the form of lost gas mileage, adding up to much more than the cost of new parts.

As mentioned in Chapter 8, check the timing twice a year and adjust if necessary. Timing is all-important. If the spark is timed to come too early, pre-ignition will result. If the spark is timed to come too late, poor engine power and low gas mileage will result.

The other part of the ignition system that might require periodic care is the alternator. Alternators generate the electricity to run the car, just as large generators produce electricity in power plants. The alternator is connected to the engine crankshaft by a fan belt. The fan belt turns the rotor of the alternator through the pulley shaft on the alternator to generate electricity. A defective alternator can very quickly drain a battery. Any indication of faulty alternator operation should be investigated immediately. Dashboard warning lights or gauges provide warning signals of impending trouble (Fig. 9-9).

At the first sign of trouble, test the alternator or other auxiliary ignition system equipment using the proper equipment and methods outlined in the shop manual. Normally the alternator will last 100,000 miles with little or no service. To keep it in top shape, there are some things you can do.

Check and adjust the alternator belt tension every month. A belt that is too loose or glazed will slip on the pulley and slow down the turning of the alternator, with subsequent loss of electric generating capacity. A belt that is too tight can cause premature wear of the alternator bearings. Adjust the belt to the proper tension recommended. Alternator brushes capture the ac current generated in the alternator through the slip rings. This current must be changed from ac to dc. Diodes take the current from the brushes and change it to dc for use by the ignition system. They eventually wear down, however, and will need to be replaced, especially if you are planning to keep your car for more than 100,000 miles. The cost of replacement is minimal. Replace whenever the brushes are worn past the indicator marked on the brushes or at 100,000 miles, whichever comes first. At the same time, clean the slip rings in solvent and lightly sand with 3/0 paper. Refer to the shop manual. If the rings are in poor condition, replace the entire slip ring assembly. Also, at 50,000 miles, consider running the alternator through the series of tests outlined in the shop manual. Correct any deficiencies found in the alternator.

Fig. 9-9. Alternator.

STARTERS

The starter is simply an electric motor used to turn the engine for starting. The starter, like the alternator, normally lasts a long time without major service. The starter is activated by a switch, called a solenoid, that is usually mounted directly on the starter case. The starter motor turns the flywheel of the engine via a pinion gear on the starter shaft. When the engine fires, the starter pinion gear disengages from the flywheel. Because the starter motor must handle large torque to turn the engine, it should be serviced slightly sooner than the alternator—perhaps at every 75,000 miles (Fig. 9-10).

There are no warning lights or gauges to indicate starter troubles as there are for alternator troubles. There are some symptoms to watch out for, however. If the starter spins freely without turning the engine, the pinion gear has not engaged the flywheel. Inspect for worn pinion gear or flywheel gear teeth, or a defective starter overrun clutch. A slow-cranking engine normally points to an electrical problem such as poor electrical contact at cable terminations, a weak solenoid, or a defective starter relay. Engines that crank noisily are usually caused by a poor mesh of pinion-to-flywheel gear teeth. Sometimes this is caused by a loosely mounted starter or worn or missing gear teeth. If the engine will not crank at all, check first for open circuits. Follow the procedure in the shop manual. Here's a tip: If your car has a seat belt interlock system and it's defective, the engine won't crank.

Inspect the starter brushes every 75,000 miles. Replace as needed. Clean and polish the commutator at this time, also. At 75,000 miles, run the starter through the series of tests outlined in the shop manual. Correct any deficiencies found in the starter. For both the alternator and starter, it is important to consult the shop manual for service and tests because these components vary greatly in design from one manufacturer to another.

Fig. 9-10. Starter.

ELECTRONIC IGNITION

Electronic ignition systems do the same job as the breaker point ignition systems. They differ only in the way the current to the primary coil winding is switched on and off, and that they have an electronic control unit. Instead of the breaker points, most electronic ignition distributors have a magnetic pulsing system that triggers the electronic control unit to interrupt the current flow to the primary coil winding. From this point on the electronic ignition system functions exactly as the breaker point system. The coil produces a high-voltage current in the secondary winding, which flows through the ignition cable to the cap, rotor, and eventually the spark plug. Figure 9-11 is a simplified schematic of a typical electronic ignition system showing the alternator, ignition switch, coil, electronic control unit, and the distributor. The electronic control unit takes the place of the breaker points in this system.

The electronic ignition system uses transistors to switch the current flow on and off through the primary winding of the coil instead of the mechanical breaker points. The advantages of the transistorized system are obvious. There are no moving parts to wear or adjust. There are no points that could pit or burn, and transistors can handle much higher voltage and current than breaker points. This allows use of a bigger spark across the spark plug gap, resulting in increased ignition efficiency and less plug fouling. These higher ignition voltages have made it possible for designers to lean the air-fuel mixture for better gas mileage and pollution control. And because of these higher voltages, all

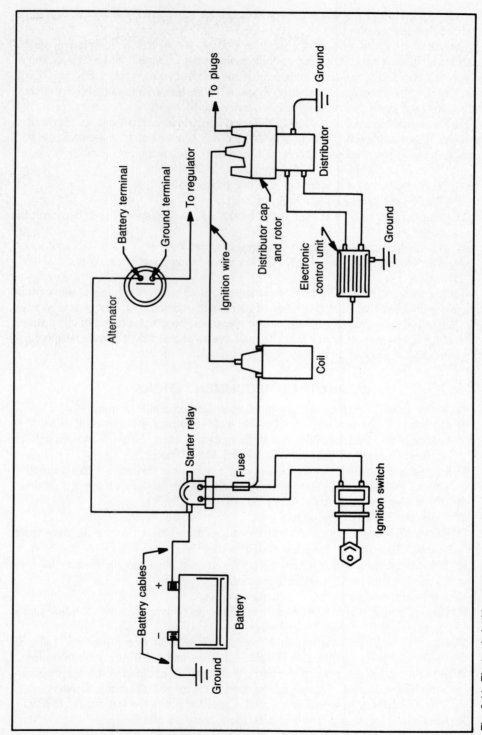

Fig. 9-11. Electronic ignition system.

Battery terminal

Ground terminal

To regulator

Alternator

To plugs

Ground

Distributor

Distributor cap and rotor

Ignition wire

Electronic control unit

Ground

Coil

Starter relay

Fuse

Ignition switch

Battery cables

+

−

Battery

Ground

electronic ignition system cabling is made with insulation formulated with silicone to provide better insulating properties.

The distributor cap, the rotor, and the ignition wires are the only parts of the electronic ignition system requiring periodic maintenance. Inspect and service them in the same manner and at the same interval as in the breaker point system. Every 100,000 miles, run the electronic ignition system through the series of tests outlined in the shop manual. Replace parts out of specification, as required.

Each manufacturer uses a slightly different electronic control unit or distributor assembly. Explaining each of them is not within our scope, but as a general rule you may suspect electronic ignition problems if one of the following five conditions occur:

1. The engine will not start but turns over normally.
2. The engine backfires and will not start.
3. The engine misfires at high speed or stalls at normal speed, and then can't be restarted.
4. The engine runs roughly at low speeds or at idle.
5. The engine runs when cold, but when hot, runs roughly or stalls.

Consult the shop manual for tests you can perform to isolate the cause of these problems. Keep in mind that heat is a killer of electronic components. Every few months check for any dirt or grease build-up on the electronic control unit that might insulate it. If cooling air cannot get to the unit, it could overheat and fail. It should be mounted away from all hot engine parts.

SUMMARY OF RECOMMENDATIONS

■ Never crank a cold engine for more than 30 seconds at a time.
■ Recharge the battery as you notice signs of weakening. Keep it at or above 75% charge at all times. Consider trickle charging in winter. Consider use of a battery or engine heater to help prolong battery life in winter.
■ Inspect and clean battery terminals twice a year. Coat terminals with a protective jelly or grease to fight corrosion. Also inspect the battery cables at this time.
■ Check battery water level every month.
■ Clean the battery case once a year.
■ Check, clean, and tighten all electrical connections before every tune-up or twice a year. Also inspect cable insulation at this time.
■ Replace ignition cables when worn with aramid fibre, or shielded metal wire conductor cable with silicone insulation.
■ Perform a cable resistance test twice a year.
■ Inspect and gap spark plugs at every tune-up or twice a year. Replace spark plugs every 12,000 to 15,000 miles.
■ Inspect the distributor assembly twice a year or at every tune-up. Lube all necessary parts at this time. Replace the cap and rotor every 50,000 miles.
■ Run the alternator through the battery of tests, as outlined in the shop manual, every 50,000 miles. Service as required. Replace the alternator brushes every 100,000 miles or sooner, if warranted. Clean and polish the slip rings at this time.
■ Check and adjust alternator belt tension every month.

- Run the starter through the battery of tests, as outlined in the shop manual, every 75,000 miles. Service as required. Replace the brushes every 100,000 miles or sooner, if warranted. Clean the commutator at this time.
- Clean the electronic control unit housing every few months. Brush clean with a dry brush only, do not use any liquid or solvent.

MECHANIC'S TIPS

- Make sure the battery hold-down bolts or bracket is in good shape and tight.
- Clean and, if necessary, paint the battery tray every year.
- Buy name brand spark plugs only. Bargain brands won't last and won't transmit the needed spark for best performance.
- When installing spark plugs, torque them to factory specifications. If you overtighten them, especially in aluminum engines, you risk stripping the threads in the engine. Repair is expensive.
- Keep grease, oil, and dirt off the spark cables. Sometimes grease and dirt will cause spark crossover between adjacent wires with resultant loss of performance.
- Patch distributor cracks with special non-conductive silicone patch or replace as soon as possible to prevent loss of spark.

10

An Integrated Tune-Up

A TUNE-UP IS THE PROCESS BY WHICH ALL MECHANICAL, ELECTRICAL/ELECTRONIC, CHEM-ical, and fluid dynamic systems (both liquid and gaseous) are returned to normal condition in order to bring engine performance to its optimum level. Car systems wear or suffer loss of adjustment due to such things as heat, vibration, etc. We need to periodically restore these systems to keep our cars at peak performance.

GENERAL PROCEDURE

If you have not established a tune-up schedule for your car, learn to look for and recognize the signs that tip you off that service is needed. Keep a record of your fuel mileage. When it begins to drop off, a tune-up is probably needed. Learn the "response" of your car. If it doesn't accelerate as rapidly or as smoothly as usual, perhaps a tune-up is just the thing that's needed for the car and your peace of mind as well.

Tune-ups are easy to perform even on today's complex cars. Easy, however, doesn't imply that doing sloppy or careless work will get the job done. To get maximum benefit and performance from a tune-up, accuracy and precision are required. To do a good tune-up, a carefully planned sequence of tests and adjustments must be performed. Every system must be checked in order and proper adjustments or parts replacement made without exception for optimum results. The advantages in proceeding this way are twofold.

First, by following a prescribed sequence, trouble spots cannot be easily overlooked. Use a checklist. That way, if the next item on the list is spark plugs, for example, only by deliberately skipping them would you fail to look at and adjust or clean them. Second, the correct adjustment of some tune-up items depends on whether previous checklist items were done correctly or even at all. As an example, adjusting a carburetor before properly setting the timing is generally a waste of time. The timing needs to be adjusted before any adjustments to the carburetor can successfully be made.

Proper and timely tune-ups are the car owner's solution to the "pay me now or pay me later" dilemma advertised so well on television. Tune-ups faithfully performed can reduce future repair bills because minor problems are caught before they become major problems. And that's doubly important for those of us who do mostly city stop-and-go driving. In this case, the engine might not reach operating temperature quickly or even at all on very short trips, causing valves to stick, compression to drop, etc.

Some tips are in order before proceeding. First, never tune up a car in a closed garage. With the engine running, carbon monoxide fumes can build quickly and strike suddenly. You might not even realize you're about to be overcome; you'll simply pass out. You could die within minutes.

Next, make sure you know what you're doing. Review the shop manual section on tune-ups the night before the tune-up. If you still feel uneasy, ask a knowledgeable friend to help out. Doing an improper tune-up is worse, in most cases, than not doing one at all. And remember those vocational-technical courses at night school; they provide professional training at low cost.

Practice makes perfect. Practice and become familiar with all your test instruments and equipment. Know what meters or gauges to use to perform tests or checks. Just reading the instructions that come with the instruments and equipment is usually not enough, unless you already have broad knowledge and experience doing tune-ups. It normally is necessary to review the shop manual to discover what instruments or equipment to use for a particular tune-up or service function. If any of the instruments are battery-operated, make sure the batteries are in good shape before you plan to use them.

Familiarize yourself with the tune-up specifications for your car and have them handy. The shop manual will have a list of them. They are the values of such things as spark plug gap (in inches or millimeters), idle speed settings, alternator output, timing settings, etc. To provide your car with a good tune-up, you must adhere to all the specifications as closely as possible.

Lastly, don't wait until Saturday morning to run down all the parts you will need. There is no better way to kill your enthusiasm for doing any work on your car than by wasting time tracking down parts at the last minute. Make a parts list the weekend before you plan to do the tune-up. Then spend some leisurely time during the week gathering the parts together. You'll have time to check the newspaper for auto store rates and time to make any special trips to pick up parts from the dealer or maybe the junk yard. What a terrific feeling it will be to face Saturday morning with a complete set of tune-up parts.

THE CORRECT STEPS

Stick to the following sequence for the tune-up work. The benefits, as explained above, will be obvious.

The Battery

1. Remove the battery cables from the battery terminals.
2. Inspect the case, cable vent caps, clamps, and holder. Clean and/or repair as necessary.

3. Install the cables.
4. Perform the specific gravity and electrical tests outlined in the service manual.
5. Recharge or replace the battery as necessary.

Engine Compression

1. Perform an engine compression test following the instructions in the service manual.
2. It doesn't make much sense to proceed further if the engine shows signs of poor compression. Have the engine repaired to bring the compression up to specification before the next step.

Electrical Connections and Tests

1. Check all important electrical connections for tightness and continuity.
2. Clean or replace any connectors found faulty.
3. Some connections to check are:

   ☐ All battery cable connections to battery and engine or starter solenoid.
   ☐ All ignition cables.
   ☐ Any wiring to the carburetor.
   ☐ All distributor wiring.
   ☐ Gauge wiring such as temperature and pressure of the engine.
   ☐ Wiring and connections to relays, alternators, generators and starters.

4. Check all fuses and circuit breakers according to the instructions in the service manual.
5. Replace any frayed, oil-soaked, or torn wires or cables before proceeding.
6. Check the alternator, regulator, and ignition coil for proper output and resistance via the directions in the service manual.

Mechanical Checks

1. Check the torque of the cylinder head bolts. If they require tightening, torque them to the value and according to the sequence in the service manual.
2. Check and, if necessary, tighten the intake and exhaust manifold bolts to the torque values in the service manual.
3. Properly torque the base of the carburetor to the intake manifold. Check for leaks following directions in the service manual. Repair leaks before proceeding.
4. Check and tighten the fuel and vacuum connections at the carburetor and fuel pump (if mechanical type).
5. If the car is equipped with a manifold heat control valve make sure it is free to move. Otherwise, free it with penetrating oil.

V-Belts

1. Inspect all the V-belts for wear and tension.
2. Replace any belts at this time. Note: It's not worth the risk to try to get a few

more miles out of a worn V-belt. If it fails while you're on the road, you'll be stuck. Replace V-belts at the very first signs of trouble.

Cooling System

1. Check all heater hoses, radiator hoses, and hoses to the carburetor or other equipment. Replace as necessary.
2. Inspect the radiator for signs of corrosion. Repair if needed.
3. Check the thermostat. Replace if necessary.
4. Check the radiator cap. Replace if necessary.
5. Inspect the overflow hose and overflow tank. Replace the hose and/or clean the tank, if necessary.
6. Remove dead bugs and other debris from the radiator.
7. Make sure the entire cooling system is leak-free. Repair any leaks before proceeding.

Air Cleaner

1. Replace all the air filters on the engine. There might be two or three of them. Refer to the service manual.
2. With the main air filter off and the engine running, spray some carburetor cleaner into the carburetor. Repeat this until the inside of the carburetor looks clean.
3. If the engine uses an oil-wetted or oil-bath main air filter, refer to the service manual for proper maintenance.

Pollution Control System (PCS)

We cover four systems here.

(Warning: in some states you cannot legally perform tune-up services on a car unless you are licensed to do so by the state.)

1. Positive Crankcase Ventilation (PCV)—Check the PCV valve for proper operation. It can't be cleaned, replace it if it doesn't move freely. Refer to the service manual.
2. Exhaust Gas Recirculation (EGR)—Check the operation of the EGR valve according to the instructions in the service manual. Some models can be cleaned. Otherwise, replace them. A dirty EGR valve will affect engine performance.
3. Air Injection or Thermactor System—This system promotes more complete burning of exhaust gases and, therefore, reduces the carbon monoxide and hydrocarbon content of the exhaust gases. It does this by pumping fresh air under pressure into the exhaust manifold, which helps burn any unburned fuel, resulting in further oxidation of the fuel. The system is made up of the following parts: A belt-driven air pump; an air filter located on the air pump behind the drive pulley wheel; air delivery hoses; a check valve in the hose between the air pump and exhaust manifold; an air distribution manifold located on the exhaust manifold or internally within the exhaust manifold; a bypass valve that acts both as a pressure relief valve and a shut-off valve on low vacuum.

The Thermactor System usually performs trouble-free. Service it during the tune-up as follows:

- [ ] Remove the air delivery hose and start the engine.
- [ ] Check for air flow through the hose.
- [ ] Inspect and tighten drive belts to specification.
- [ ] Using soapy water, check for air leaks around the air filter and at all connections. Repair if necessary.
- [ ] Inspect the check valve. Remove it and try blowing through it in the opposite direction—back toward the air pump. If you can blow through, it's defective and needs to be replaced.

4. Evaporative Control System (ECS)—this system is designed to control the leakage of fuel vapors to atmosphere. American Motors, General Motors, and Ford use a charcoal storage system to absorb fuel vapors. Other manufacturers use a crankcase system requiring no maintenance. If your car has a crankcase system you can proceed beyond this step. The charcoal-based systems are made up of the following parts: a charcoal storage unit, an air filter usually located at the bottom of the charcoal storage unit, a special fuel tank cap, and tubing lines.

The ECS system usually performs trouble-free. Service it as follows:

- [ ] Make sure all tubing is in good condition and tight.
- [ ] Replace the air filter element.
- [ ] Check the fuel tank cap for leaks. Refer to the service manual. Replace the cap if it's damaged or lost.
- [ ] Unclog any tubing lines that are restricted.

Spark Plugs

1. Remove all the plugs and inspect them for signs of engine trouble.
2. Clean and regap the plugs, if necessary.
3. If the plugs are too worn, replace them.
4. Reinstall the plugs, being careful not to strip threads, and make sure the correct cables are installed on each plug.
5. At the end of this step, check the manifold vacuum for proper value according to the procedure in the service manual.

Distributor and Timing

1. Remove and clean the distributor cap and rotor. Make sure the cap is not cracked.
2. Replace the cap if it's cracked and the rotor if the copper contact is worn, pitted, or corroded.
3. If the car uses breaker points, clean and adjust them. Replace if the points are pitted or burned.

4. Check the breaker point spring tension and adjust, if necessary.
5. Lubricate according to the service manual instructions.
6. Reassemble carefully.
7. Check and adjust the timing to specification. The service manual will provide complete instructions.

Fuel System

1. Clean the carburetor sediment bowl and fuel filters. Given their low cost, replace the fuel filters rather than cleaning them. In-line fuel filters must be replaced, they cannot be cleaned.
2. Clean and adjust all the carburetor linkage and the choke mechanism.
3. Make sure the fuel pump works properly. Tests are outlined in the service manual.

Exhaust System

1. Check the muffler(s), catalytic converter(s), and pipes for damage and leakage.
2. Make sure the system is tight and doesn't bounce around when the car is moving.

Note: Consider changing the oil and oil filter, and performing a grease job at tune-up time to top off a good job.

Road Test

1. Drive the car under all normal driving conditions for 15 to 20 minutes. Be sensitive to things like uneven acceleration or engine misses. Recheck trouble areas, if necessary.
2. Check for oil, fuel, and coolant leaks.

SUMMARY OF RECOMMENDATIONS

- Perform a tune-up faithfully twice a year.
- Keep a record of fuel mileage. When it begins to drop off a tune-up may be in order.
- Perform the tune-up according to a sequence of events.
- Never tune up a car in a closed garage; carbon monoxide poisoning may result.
- Become knowledgeable about tune-ups. Study the service manual or take a course at the local vocational school or community college.
- Familiarize yourself with your tools and test equipment.
- Have a complete set of tune-up specifications at ready reference.
- Gather all the replacement parts you think will be needed before you start to work. Don't wait until the last minute to hunt down parts.

MECHANIC'S TIPS

- Mark spring-type clothes pins with cylinder numbers and then snap them on the spark plug wires in order not to lose track of which wires go where. Remember to remove them before operating the car.

■ Use a fender cover when leaning over the car. And don't wear a belt with a metal buckle because it could scratch the paint on the fender.

■ Consider cleaning the engine with degreaser before you perform a tune-up.

■ To better read the appropriate timing marks of the timing pulley, etch them with a dab of phosphorescent paint. They will show up nicely in the light of the timing gun.

■ Have plenty of rags available. Keep your hands clean, especially when working with electrical parts. Consider using a pair of light cotton gloves as added dirt protection.

11

Car Body Care

TO PROPERLY MAINTAIN A CAR INVOLVES WASHING, WAXING, AND SCRUBBING THE INTERIOR and exterior, as well as repairing and maintaining all the numerous mechanical parts. There is a trade-off: You can wash the car once or twice a year and accept the rusty consequences. You can allow the sand, dirt and dust to pile up inside the car to the point where going to church on Sunday requires wearing an old fashioned duster like your great-grandfather used. Or you can invest in a handful of cleaners and waxes and, with a little elbow grease, keep your car looking showroom new.

INSIDE

Interior upholstery in modern cars is available in cloth and vinyl materials, and sometimes in leather. Each of these requires different kinds of care and cleaning methods. Upholstery includes the seat and door coverings, the floormat or carpet, and the headliner.

Cloth and Velour Interiors

Cloth upholstery requires the most care of the three types commercially available. Most people select cloth interiors for its warmth, comfort, and pleasing appearance. This benefit must be traded off against the increased care required compared to vinyl upholstery.

Modern cloth upholstery is tough and stain resistant. It still collects dust, dirt, and grease, however, and will show wear much earlier than vinyl upholstery. A good tip on caring for cloth interiors is to treat them just like the furniture in the house. You wouldn't sit on your living room couch with dirty trousers or walk across your $25-per-square-yard rug with muddy shoes, would you?

Clean cloth upholstery at least once every month or sooner, depending on frequency and type of use. Brush the upholstery with a medium stiff bristle brush to loosen stubborn, abrasive dirt. After brushing, vacuum the entire interior. When you're sure the car interior is clean, consider applying one of the commercially available stain guards to protect the upholstery.

Stain guard penetrates the cloth fibers, creating a coating that keeps stain out of contact with the cloth. Remember that the upholstery must still be cleaned periodically, even though stain guard has been applied. Stain guard doesn't repluse dirt, just stains.

Once or twice a year wash the upholstery with a nonalkaline soap and water solution. Apply sparingly. Don't get carried away using a lot of suds and water. Don't use laundry soap or bleach; they may discolor the cloth fabric. Auto stores sell upholstery soaps in liquid, powder, and spray forms that are correctly formulated for cloth upholstery use. Check them out.

Cloth fabrics in modern cars are made of synthetic yarns, typically rayon and nylon. Some of these materials are also foam-backed. The foam can be dissolved by some of the volatile cleaners on the market that are used for spot or stain removal. If removing a spot or stain, stick with the type recommended by the dealer or factory and follow directions. Never use gasoline or powerful solvents like paint thinner, acetone, or nail polish remover. Gasoline is dangerous stuff and can also stain the cloth—especially leaded gasoline. The other solvents are not so dangerous, but might still weaken or dissolve the synthetic fabric. Use volatile cleaners of the approved type outdoors, with the car door open for proper ventilation. Don't breath any of the fumes, they are poisonous. Refer to Table 11-1 for some stain removal tips.

Velour interiors are perhaps the most touchy. Velour is a delicate fabric that requires professional cleaning only. Other than vacuuming, don't attempt to clean velour yourself. Keep a covering over the velour seats for added protection.

Vinyl Interiors

Vinyl interiors are much more rugged and are easier to maintain than cloth interiors. Granted, vinyl seats are not as comfortable in the winter cold or summer heat as cloth seats. However, ease of maintenance of vinyl is a great benefit.

Vinyl is actually a thermoplastic. Thermoplastic polymers can be remelted at between 212 to 570 degrees Fahrenheit, so in most cases the vinyl in your car can be repaired via a heat process. Tears can also be repaired by gluing.

Vinyl is very susceptible to fading from sunshine. The ultraviolet rays bleach the surface of the vinyl and, over time, cause it to harden and crack. A garage-kept car or one with seat covers is shielded against these harmful rays. There are a few conditioners available on the market for sun protection. They keep the vinyl soft and provide some protection against dirt penetration and ultraviolet rays. Investigate their use.

As stated above, vinyl upholstery is easier to clean than cloth upholstery. It does get dirty, however, because its surface is covered with tiny pores that trap dirt and grease. Clean monthly with mild soap or a commercial vinyl cleaner. Vacuum first to remove loose dirt.

Vinyl is extremely susceptible to strong detergents or cleaning fluids. And remember it scratches and tears easily, so don't use abrasives to clean it. Use only approved cleaners for removing stains. Any other cleaning fluid may discolor, wrinkle, or dissolve the vinyl

Table 11-1. Stain Removal.

Stain	Cleaning Method
Ball point	1. Rubbing alcohol, repeated applications. If no results:
Ink	2. Apply vaseline. Flush with carbon tetrachloride. Avoid ink eradicator.
Blood	1. Rub with cold water (hot water sets the stain). If no results: 2. Rub with household ammonia.
Candy	1. Rub with warm water. If no results: 2. Use approved volatile cleaner.
Catsup	1. Rub with cold water. If no results: 2. Use mild soap solution.
Chewing Gum	1. Apply ice to harden gum and scrape. If no results: 2. Use approved volatile cleaner.
Coffee	1. Rub with cold water only. If no results: 2. Use approved volatile cleaner. Don't use soap, it may set the stain.
Chocolate	See "Candy"
Cream/Milk	See "Coffee"
Fruit	See "Coffee"
Ice Cream	See "Coffee"
Lipstick	1. Use approved volatile cleaner only.
Liquor	See "Coffee"
Mustard	1. Rub with warm water, then with mild detergent. Repeat as necessary.
Shoe Polish	1. Use approved volatile cleaner.
Tar	1. Scrape off as much as possible, then use approved volatile cleaner.
Urine	1. Rub gently with soap solution. Rinse with cold water. Lift stain by applying cloth soaked in 20% ammonia solution for a minute or two.
Vomit	1. Rub gently with cold water. Then wash with warm soap solution. To remove odor, use a baking soap solution.

and ruin it. Before using any cleaners, try picking off the dirt or a stain with masking tape. Sometimes the adhesive on the tape will lift the spot, saving a lot of aggravation.

Leather Interiors

Not many cars are available—or, we should say, affordable—with leather interiors. For those of you who can afford it, leather is a superb material. It's soft, supple, and it breathes—no sticky or wet seats in the summer. Leather doesn't need much more attention than cloth or vinyl, although preventive maintenance is well worth the investment and effort.

Leather should be vacuumed monthly. Clean it with saddle soap or a good-quality leather creme. Keep in mind that leather is an animal skin and will dry out and crack with age. Once cracking starts, it is just about impossible to stop it. To keep the leather soft and supple, apply one of the commercially available leather conditioners to prolong its life. Follow the manufacturer's directions and recommended frequency of application.

Repairs

Loose seams or/tears in any upholstery material should be repaired as soon as possible. Small repairs left undone have a way of becoming major repairs in no time at all.

Cloth upholstery can be sewn quite successfully, as long as tears or rips aren't too large. Use a tight X-pattern cross-stitch for repairs. Cotton or nylon thread can be used. Don't pull the nylon thread too tight; it might cut the cloth fabric. Pulled-apart seams are the easiest repair to make. Tie off the ends that are torn or loose and stitch the open seam back about an inch beyond the tied-off ends. This adds strength to the stitch. It shouldn't come apart again. For more involved repairs, visit an upholstery shop or consult an upholstery repair book.

Vinyl repairs are much more complicated than cloth fabric repairs, but can be done by the novice. Small tears and rips can be repaired by gluing and patching. Place a patch of the same vinyl material underneath the tear and on top of the padding, if on a seat. Cut the patch so that it is about ¼ inch larger in perimeter than the tear. Apply vinyl cement to the patch and the tear and press together. Use a vinyl repair kit to finish the edges.

Seam openings in vinyl can be repaired using a soldering iron equipped with a curved tip. Insert the tip in the seam, heating both sides of the split. Press the joint together to bond it. Be careful not to overheat the vinyl when doing this repair.

Repairs in leather and velour are for professionals to handle. You'll only make the problem worse if you attempt any repairs. Have velour and leather repaired as soon as possible.

Furthermore teach your children not to abuse your car's interior. Tell them the car furniture is just like the house furniture; no jumping, kicking, or fooling around on it. If you allow your children to have food in the car and they spill it, it's your fault—don't punish them. Just clean the mess as soon as possible.

Pets probably won't spill ice cream or pizza unless you can teach them to hold it in their paws. Pets have claws, however, that will quickly ruin any type of upholstery and they do get car sick. Also, pet hair is a chore to clean up. Leave the pet at home or, if possible, transport it in a pet carrying cage.

OUTSIDE

Then there's the guy who washes his car once a year whether it needs it or not. He uses abrasive cleanser to make sure all the dirt is gone. He says you don't need to do anything else to keep the exterior looking good. And, oh yes, he says a $150 paint job is a must every couple of years to "tone it up!"

Maintaining the exterior of your car should be nothing like the story above. It takes a lot of scheduled work and some elbow grease now and then. With the proper care your car can be free of rust and shine, and showroom-new for years and years. Just knowing the proper cleaners (nothing abrasive) and waxes and when to use them is most of the battle.

Exterior Finishes

Cars manufactured today use two basic types of paint: enamel and lacquer. Enamel takes about six months to fully cure to form the characteristically tough, hard finish, while lacquer takes almost no time at all to cure.

Enamel will dry harder and smoother than lacquer and will look glossier. The liquid portion of enamel paint, called the vehicle, is a varnish instead of an oil. Varnish gives the enamel its hardness and smoothness. The varnish can be a spar varnish, a shellac varnish, or a catalytic varnish used to produce a solid, film coating.

Two types of enamel in common use are acrylic enamel and polyurethane enamel. Acrylic is a hardening agent. If it is mixed with enamel, the resultant mix dries to a harder consistency than plain enamel. Polyurethane is an artificial rubber-based polymer. When it is added to enamel it lends both hardness and toughness, or durability. It is a premium paint and, although costly, should be seriously considered when purchasing a new car or at repainting time.

Lacquer is made from a resinous secretion, called lac, of an insect living on the sap of certain trees. The lac is refined and combined with alcohol to make a spirit or shellac varnish. It is then further combined with cellulose nitrate or cellulose acetate butyrate to form lacquer. Because of the way lacquer is formulated, it can be dissolved by paint thinner even if it has been on the car for years. If your car has a lacquer paint job don't go near it with paint thinner—ever!

Lacquer can also be combined with acrylic to form a finish harder than lacquer alone. In fact, acrylic lacquer is harder than acrylic enamel, although not as durable.

When repainting, you need to be cautious about what types of new paint you use over the old paint already on the car. If the car is sanded down to bare metal you can apply any type of paint your heart desires. However, new paint applied over old paint performs satisfactorily only in certain combinations: When using lacquer over factory enamel, the results will be poor to fair. Enamel over lacquer, however, usually gives good results. The worst combination is lacquer over paint shop baked enamel. The results are disasterous. Paint shop baked enamel is baked at 150 degrees Fahrenheit, whereas factory baked enamel is baked at 350 degrees Fahrenheit. Lacquer sprayed over a paint shop baked enamel will penetrate the enamel and eventually cause it to peel. Stay away from that combination. For excellent results, consider sanding the paint down to bare metal, doing any necessary repairs, and then painting with any type of good quality paint, lacquer or enamel.

Cleaning

The only way to prevent rust and corrosion is to keep your car clean and dry. Cleaning involves washing, waxing, and spot removal. Keeping your car dry involves wiping after washing and sealing the car against water intrusion.

Washing. Wash your car weekly. Stick to this schedule even when it hurts to do so. In warm weather, rise early on a Saturday morning before anyone else and get it done. In winter take it to a car wash, if you must. Remember, though, that the soap used at a carwash is extremely caustic; it needs to be in order to remove road grime by spraying only. It's better to wash your car yourself.

Wash your car with mild soap and warm water. You can use a commercially prepared car wash soap (without wax) or dishwashing liquid. In any case, use something mild that rinses well and doesn't leave a film. Find a shady spot under which to wash the car. You want to keep the sunlight from drying the soapy water too fast to avoid streaking.

Before you begin washing, spray the car down mildly to remove loose surface dirt. Use a soft, porous sponge that will soak up the dirt in its pores. A rag will only drag the dirt across the surface and scratch it. Use a light to mild pressure to do the actual washing. Buy a fender brush and be sure to wash the wheel wells with it. Road dirt and salt have a nasty habit of accumulating in the wheel wells. Also, remember to wash the door jambs and the splash pans under the bumpers.

Rinse your car with water, paying particular attention to the wheel wells, behind bumpers, and any other secret places where dirt and water can hide. Dry the car with a soft cloth or chamois.

Waxing. Car waxes come in two types: natural and synthetic. Natural car wax is a composition of oils, beeswax, and carnauba wax. Synthetic wax is a blend of synthetic polymers with silicone added. Synthetic wax is harder than carnauba-based natural wax and will protect painted surfaces longer. Many car buffs, however, prefer to use the carnauba-based waxes. Some use 100% carnauba wax. Natural or synthetic, either choice will work. Just keep in mind that you might have to wax more often with the natural wax.

Waxes are also available as a paste or liquid. Car buffs prefer the paste wax, but the liquid does a fine job, too. You can buy waxes combined with cleaners, but we advise against them. The cleaners could contain abrasives that might scratch or dull the car finish with repeated use. Better stick with the plain paste or liquid wax.

Oxygen in the air acts, over time, to oxidize the surface layer of paint on the car. Waxing removes much of the oxidation layer that washing alone cannot. In addition, the wax leaves a coating that helps prevent future oxidation, and also keeps dust and dirt away from the paint. And if you cannot park your car indoors, the ultraviolet rays of the sunshine will, in time, fade the paint. Waxing screens out these rays to some extent.

Wax will eventually wear off and will have to be replaced. Plan to wax your car every month or two. This might sound like a lot of time and work, but some of the newer liquid waxes on the market go on and come off easily. The time spent should only involve a few hours each month or two and is well worth it.

Here are some waxing hints: First, follow the directions that come with the wax. Some waxes are temperature sensitive, others need to be applied with a dry cloth or wet cloth. Don't' use a power buffer when waxing. Too much pressure will wear both wax and paint away. Elbow grease works best. Always wax in the shade and wax all the car surfaces except the tires and windows. You may consider using a special cleaner and polish for the chrome surfaces on the car. Never wax windows to clean them. Use a commercial spray window cleaner and wipe dry with newspaper or a soft, absorbent towel or rag.

Cars with vinyl or convertible tops are a special problem. The surface of vinyl and convertible tops are very porous and act as terrific dirt collectors. You need to wash and coat these tops three or four times per year. Buy the special cleaner available for these tops and brush it in with a semi-stiff brush, making sure to loosen all the dirt. This might take some effort on your part. After the top is clean and completely dry, coat it with a dressing or conditioner made for the material. Follow directions closely.

Sealing. Your car comes from the factory sealed against water intrusion from rain and road splashing. Over time the trim around doors, windows, hoods, and trunks vibrates loose or the trim cement holding weatherstripping dries out. Water can then find its way into the inside of doors, panels, and the interior of the car. To head off rust, you need to keep this water out of the car or make sure it drains out quickly through the factory designed drain holes in doors.

Seal loose trim and weatherstripping with fresh trim cement or, preferably, silicone sealant. Silicone sealant is especially useful around windshields. Make sure door drain holes are open. Check them monthly. Attend to all leaks as soon as possible.

You can test for leaks by spraying the car with water. Look for telltale water runs in the interior around doors and windows. Another way to test for leaks is to run the heater on high and feel around all the windows for escaping air. Mark every spot suspected of leaking and seal appropriately.

Wear

The basic types of body wear that car owners must concern themselves with are rust, tar, and abrasion.

Rust. The wear most prevalent on the car exterior is, of course, rust. Rust is the oxidation of iron-base materials on the body of your car. It is a type of corrosion that occurs when an iron-base material is immersed in water or water-containing salts and then exposed to the air. Most rust is actually a hydroxide of iron, called ferric hydroxide. The way to avoid rusting is to keep the car metal dry and out of contact with oxygen in the air. In all cars this is accomplished by coating all or certain highly susceptible body parts with either inorganic or organic coatings.

Inorganic coatings typically are zinc (galvanizing), chrome, copper, nickel, tin, and cadmium. Tin is most often used for body part coating. It can be applied by electrodeposition or hot dipping, and is usually applied to the underneath of body parts. Paint provides the exterior surface protection.

Organic coatings include paints, varnishes, lacquers, epoxy coatings, and epoxy-coal tar coatings. Most of these coatings are satisfactory for a number of years but will not outlast inorganic coatings. They require more care also. And don't confuse undercoating with rust protection. Undercoating is used primarily for its sound-deadening qualities—to seal out road noise. In fact, as the undercoating cracks with age, it can form pockets and crevices that trap water against the metal, accelerating the rusting process.

Rust-proofing your car can help to prolong the life of the metal body parts significantly. In this procedure, all surfaces susceptible to rusting are sprayed with an oily, waxy substance that forms a protective barrier against water, salts, and oxygen. Holes are drilled for spraying in car doors and other limited-access areas, and then plugged when the job is done. Rust-proofing is valuable only when the car is new, otherwise it is a waste of money. It's too late to apply rust-proofing after the car has been driven over wet, salt-laden roads. As soon as salt and water collect in even the smallest amounts, oxidation (rust) begins. And don't rust-proof your car yourself. Take it to a professional who offers at least a three-year guarantee against rusting.

Washing and waxing according to the recommendations offered here will go a long way in the crusade against rust. Flush out all areas where salt can collect, such as fender wells and underneath the car. And fix rust as soon as you notice it.

Tar. Road tars are part of the asphalt used to pave roadways. Asphalts are bitumens obtained from petroleum residuals as a byproduct of refining petroleum. They are somewhat susceptible to warm temperatures. On a hot day, asphalt roadways tend to soften and release road tars that collect on your car, typically at the rear of the fender wells and along the rocker panels. They are very sticky, and once dried should be removed only with special tar removers available in auto stores.

Tar tends to spot and dull the finish of your car, not to mention that it looks ugly. One way to prevent tar build-up is to install mud flaps on all four wheel wells. Years ago, cars were designed such that the areas where mud and tar were kicked up were straight up and down. Stones, mud, and tar simply dropped back to the ground. Nowadays, with the sweeping fender and wheel well designs, road debris can easily collect all along the bottom side of the car. Installing a set of small, stainless steel mud flaps will help prevent road mud and tar accumulation, and your car may last years longer. Considering the relatively small purchase price of mud flaps, they are well worth it.

Abrasion. Road dirt and dust also gradually abrade the exterior surfaces of your car. Just ask anyone who lives in the western states what a sandstorm can do to the finish on a car.

The best way to avoid abrasive wear on the car body is to change your driving habits. Don't follow other vehicles too closely, especially trucks. For safety's sake, too, this makes a lot of sense. Turning tires have a way of kicking up dirt and pebbles that can hit your car at terrific speeds—with disastrous results for your paint job or windshield. Stay at least one car length behind other vehicles for every 10 mph of car speed. If possible, avoid construction areas, dirt roads, pot-holed roads, and roads recently sanded or cindered for winter driving. You might think this advice somewhat radical. Consider that one bad scratch on an otherwise pristine finish will stick out like a sore thumb. Better be cautious than sorry.

Abrasion is usually the reason for failure of windshield wiper squeegees. Squeegees are made from different formulations of natural rubber. Natural rubber is rather soft compared to synthetic rubber blends. Therefore, it is more resilient yet more susceptible to abrasion wear. Weather, sunshine, pollution, and time all take their toll on squeegee life. Also, as the squeegee oscillates back and forth across the windshield, it drags small particles of abrasive road dirt and dust with it. These particles tend to scratch, cut, and tear the wiper surface over a length of time and gradually cause it to streak the windshield. At this point, replace the squeegee. Wash and inspect the squeegees every car wash, and replace them when necessary.

Repairs

Repairs to the exterior of the car should be made as soon as possible and be done correctly to avoid future repairs in the same area. Auto body repair is covered in great detail in a myriad of publications. If you have a lot of auto body work to do, check out one of the auto body courses at your high school extension or community college. These auto body books and courses go into great detail and cover techniques for repair, auto body construction, estimating, paint formulation, and spraying techniques. Here, we will only offer a few pointers and tips, concentrating on minor dents and rust.

Working on dents requires infinite patience. You can't proceed too hastily or you might make mistakes that are difficult or impossible to correct. Gently run your hand across suspected dents to help define the extent of the dent. Check the contours of the body part carefully to find high and low spots not easily seen.

A good auto body mechanic gradually taps and pulls the metal back to its original shape, being careful not to stretch the metal any more than it already is. Smaller dents (less than $\frac{1}{8}$ inch deep) can be filled with plastic body filler. They don't normally need to be pulled or hammered out.

After the dent is pulled or hammered out, it must be ground and sanded as smooth as possible down to bright metal. This will remove paint, rust, and sharp metal before priming or filling. The next step is to apply filler and sand smooth, using your hands to gauge correct contour. Then comes the primer paint, finish paint, and waxing.

When you get your car, new or used, buy a small bottle or spray can of touch-up paint formulated to match the color of your car. You'll be using it often. If your car is more than six or seven years old, buy a supply of a few bottles or cans of paint, because most manufacturers only mix paint for the more recent cars.

Use touch-up paint only for the smallest nicks and scratches. The paint will not match exactly because the original paint on the car fades from the sun. However, these small repairs won't be noticed unless you're right on top of them. Small knicks and scratches will not rust if you touch them up as soon as you notice them.

Here is the general procedure for touch-up work: Cut away loose or blistered paint around the rust spot. Bevel the edges of the paint around the spot for better blending of the touch-up paint with the original paint. Scrape off any loose rust, being careful not to scratch any good paint. For a really professional job, apply a metal conditioner over the bare metal. It will etch the metal and any rust left, and will aid in adhesion of the primer. Next, dab some primer on the spot. Let it dry and finish with the touch-up paint.

Take care of these little rust spots promptly. If you leave them go, they can develop rather quickly into rust-through—and repairing at this point is much more involved. Once metal rusts through, it is difficult or impossible to permanently fix and arrest.

SHELTER

To keep your car exterior looking great you need to shelter it from the sun, rain, and snow as much as possible. A car kept in a dry, dark place away from dirt and the elements would look showroom-new even after 50 years. Unless your car is in a museum, you can't protect it totally 24 hours a day. There are a few things you can do, however.

If you have a garage or can rent one, by all means park your car in it whenever you're not using it. If the garage is cluttered with lawn mowers, boxes, bicycles, and assorted odds and ends, you must decide its ultimate use. Is the garage a general storage depot, or is it for the car and its tools and supplies?

If you don't have access to a garage, perhaps you can arrange temporary shelter for your car. Park it along the side of the house away from the prevailing wind, or under a temporary structure consisting of poles and a roof to keep some of the elements from the car. If possible, park along less busy streets to avoid careless bumps from other drivers and to minimize mud, snow, and ice from splashing on your car. And try not to park under trees where sap could dirty the car.

Another solution is to invest in a car cover. They are available from auto mail-order houses to fit your year and model car. They fit like a glove and provide the maximum in temporary protection.

Storage

What do you do if you are not planning to use your car for several months or longer? If you park it and don't take any storage precautions, you could be doing irreparable damage to it. Rust will set in, especially in the engine and drive train as oil drains from upper engine parts to settle in the crankcase. If kept outdoors, the sun will bake the car day after day. And in cooler weather, moisture can settle out in the fuel tank and lines. Store the car in a garage and consider the following tips:

1. Drain and refill the crankcase with 10w oil. This will rid the engine of corrosive acids and sludge in the oil that can do a lot of damage over months of non-use. For the ultimate in protection, use an engine flush to clean all the internal parts before refilling with the 10w oil.
2. Don't bother draining the fuel tank unless the car will not be used for up to a year. Gasoline begins to break down after one year and shouldn't be left in the tank. Add a can of dry gas to absorb moisture.
3. Remove the battery and store it in a dry place.
4. Spray silicone lubricant in the engine compartment. This coats all the metal parts, helping to prohibit rust formation.
5. Cover all vinyl (inside and out) with drop cloths or towels.
6. Raise the car off the ground so that the weight is off the tires. Put the car on sturdy wood or concrete blocks.
7. Leave the parking brake off. Put the car in neutral or park.
8. Don't use car covers for long term storage. They trap moisture between the cover material and the car and may actually initiate or hasten rusting.

SUMMARY OF RECOMMENDATIONS

■ Clean interior surfaces at least once a month. Wash with approved cleaners once or twice a year, or as needed.
■ Use only approved spot/stain removers. Never use gasoline, paint thinner, acetone, or nail polish remover on your car interior.
■ Clean leather interiors with saddle soap or leather creme. Apply a conditioner periodically.
■ Cover velour seats for added protection.
■ Vacuum carpets every week. Shampoo them once a year.
■ Educate children in proper upholstery behavior.
■ Wash the car weekly.
■ Wax the car every month or two. Follow wax manufacturer's directions carefully. Wax in the shade. Wax everything except windows and tires. Never use a power buffer.
■ Have new cars rust-proofed.
■ Install mud flaps.
■ When driving, don't follow the vehicle in front of you too closely. This will reduce the road debris that hits your car.
■ Repair even minor dents and rust spots as soon as possible.
■ Provide appropriate shelter for your car. Store cars properly.

MECHANIC'S TIPS

■ When servicing your car, be sure to drape the seats with an old blanket or sheet to prevent the seat from being soiled by dirty or greasy trousers.
■ Take advantage of summer rain storms. Wash your car during the storm to save on water.
■ Use a hard-setting paste wax. It will last longer and shine deeper.
■ Never use abrasive cleaners on the car exterior.

12

The Cooling System

AS THE SPARK PLUG FIRES, IT IGNITES THE AIR-FUEL MIXTURE DELIVERED FROM THE INTAKE manifold during the power stroke of the engine. Ignition of the air-fuel mixture causes it to very rapidly oxidize (burn) and expand, forcing the piston downward in the cylinder. The air-fuel mixture inside the cylinder burns at temperatures approaching 4600 degrees Fahrenheit. Each firing in the cylinder does not produce that much heat because the volume of the air-fuel mixture is low. However, continued firing by four, six, or eight cylinders many times during a minute does create a rapid heat build-up.

Some of the heat produced (about 25%) is used to expand the burning air-fuel mixture. This, of course, is what drives the car as the expanding gas mixture forces the piston downward, turning the crankshaft. The balance of the heat does not do any useful work. It is passed out of the exhaust system and heats the engine oil and engine parts. The part of the heat that does not pass through the exhaust system—about 35% of the heat produced—would very quickly vaporize the lubricating oil in the cylinders and seize the engine if it were not removed from the engine. It is the job of the cooling system to remove this waste heat.

TYPES

There are two types of cooling systems in use with modern passenger cars: air and liquid. With the exception of a few imported models (and the Corvair), the great majority of car engines are liquid cooled, and these are the types of engines we shall concentrate on here.

Liquid cooling is accomplished by circulating a mixture of water and antifreeze through the passages of the water jacket inside the engine. There the heat is absorbed by the liquid mixture, which is pumped to the radiator where the cooling air flows through the radiator fins and removes the heat. The coolant liquid is circulated through the engine, hoses, and radiator by the water pump. The water pump is driven by a rubber V-belt from the crankshaft pulley and is normally located at the front of the engine.

The portions of the engine that need the most cooling are the cylinder walls and other sliding surfaces. In addition, the exhaust valves, which must handle high-temperature exhaust gases, are cooled to prevent combustion knock or overheating. In order for the piston to continue reciprocating, the cylinder walls must have a thin lubricant film for the piston rings to ride upon without cooling. High cylinder wall temperatures would quickly destroy or vaporize this oil film, causing rapid seizure of the piston rings and piston to the cylinder wall.

COMPONENTS

The major components of the cooling system are the radiator, the overflow recovery tank, the pressure cap, hoses, the thermostat, the fan, the water pump, the cylinder block passages or water jacket, the heater core, and the liquid coolant mix (antifreeze mix).

Radiator, Overflow Tank, and Pressure Cap

In the cooling system there are two primary ways heat transfer is accomplished. One is between the cooling fluid and the cylinder walls, the other between the radiator and outside air and the cooling fluid.

The radiator is a heat-transfer device. It receives heat from the hot engine coolant and transfers it to the atmosphere via the cool air moving through the radiator core (Fig. 12-1). The radiator core is made up of water tubes and connecting fins. The hot coolant

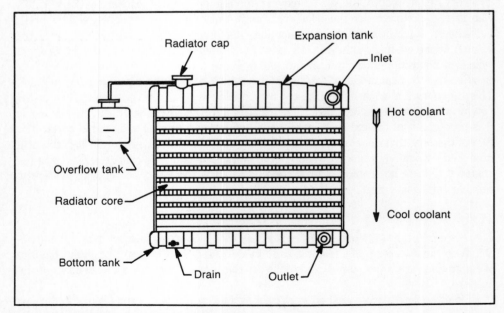

Fig. 12-1. Downflow radiator (engine side view).

flows through the water tubes from the expansion tank at the top of the radiator to the bottom tank in the radiator. As it flows downward it loses its heat through the walls of the water tubes to the fins connected to the tubes. The rate of heat transfer to the air from the fins is proportional to the surface area of the fins. To a limit, the more fins a radiator core has, the more heat it can transfer. That is why the radiator core is jammed with so much fin material.

In order to keep the heat transfer rate efficiently high, air flow around the fins and through the core must not be impeded. Clean dead insects and any road debris from the radiator core whenever you notice it. Inspect the radiator monthly. Straighten any bent fins because these will also impede air flow.

Most cars with automatic transmissions are equipped with oil coolers to cool the automatic transmission fluid. The transmission oil cooler is another, smaller, finned radiator located within the larger engine radiator. It is placed in the outlet or bottom tank of the engine radiator. The automatic transmission cooler gives up its heat to the antifreeze mix inside the radiator which, in turn, loses heat to the outside air.

Not all radiators are the downflow type described above. Downflow radiators are used on smaller engines. Another type of radiator is the crossflow type used on larger V-8 engines. It is more efficient than the downflow type and can usually be made compact enough to fit under low, sleek, hood designs. In this type of radiator, hot coolant enters the radiator at an upper right or left corner and exits at a diagonal lower corner. If there is an automatic transmission cooler, it will be located in the cooler on the exit side of the radiator (Fig. 12-2).

Most car radiators are made of brass because brass will resist rust and corrosion much better than steel. Normally, radiators give little problem, but they will corrode after a time if not properly maintained. Antifreeze contains anti-corrosion additives to forestall corrosion, but these additives wear out eventually and need to be replaced. It is therefore necessary to flush the cooling system periodically and refill with fresh

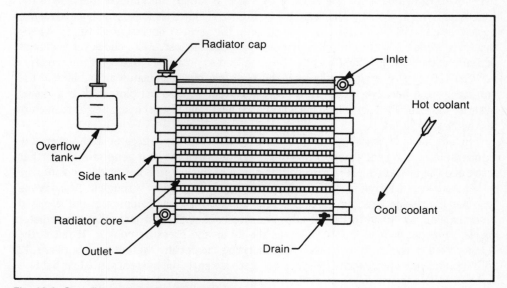

Fig. 12-2. Crossflow radiator (engine side view).

antifreeze mix. Do this every 12,000 miles. Some radiators are made of aluminum. Be sure to use antifreeze formulated for use in these radiators.

The other major radiator problem is clogging. Clogging normally occurs in the small-diameter water tubes inside the radiator. It can be caused by an accumulation of rust and corrosion scale that blocks these small holes. Periodic flushing and use of fresh antifreeze will help solve this. Clogging can also be caused by build-up of gum, sludge, and varnish deposits that are carried away from inside the engine through internal leakage of oil or burnt fuel into the cooling system. This type of clogging is rare. Suspect internal leaks where there is a gradual loss of coolant and no evidence of external leaks. Normally, internal leakage will lead to antifreeze fouling of the oil, and antifreeze leakage and burning into the cylinder, which can quickly ruin the engine. Internal leaks can be caused by a cracked intake manifold, blown head gasket, warped head, or cracked cylinder head or engine block. Repairs need to be made immediately if you suspect internal leakage.

In almost all modern cars there will be an overflow tank connected to the top of the radiator by a rubber hose. The hose is usually connected to the radiator right under the pressure cap (see Fig. 12-1). As the coolant expands from absorption of the engine heat, it forces its way past the pressure cap via a valve, through the connecting hose, and into the overflow tank. In older cars that used water instead of antifreeze as the coolant, this overflow tank wasn't necessary. Overflow simply passed through an overflow hose and spilled to the ground. Clean the overflow tank whenever it looks dirty. The overflow tank is also used to give a quick indication of coolant inventory in the cooling system. If the overflow tank is empty, it is time to check the fluid level in the radiator.

Antifreeze expands five times more than water for the same volume and the same amount of heat absorbed. Overflow was, therefore, rare with water coolant systems. However, because antifreeze expands so much more than water, we need to provide the overflow tank to capture what would otherwise be lost coolant.

When the engine is shut off, the antifreeze gradually cools and contracts and any overflow is drawn back into the radiator by a siphon action. Markings on the side of the translucent overflow tank will indicate the antifreeze liquid levels for engine hot and engine normal or shut off. Add antifreeze mix to keep the level at normal at all times. Check this level weekly. Under normal conditions no coolant is lost. Also, check for sediment or scum in the overflow tank because this can lead to potential clogging of the radiator.

Aside from preserving antifreeze, the overflow tank eliminates air bubbles in the cooling system because, in effect, a cooling system with an overflow tank is a closed system. Coolant without air bubbles will absorb heat (and lose it) much better than coolant with air bubbles.

In any heat transfer system, heat is transferred at a greater rate when the temperature of the heat absorber and the temperature of the heat generator are further apart and the system is pressurized. In the case of the car, the hotter the coolant, the faster heat is transferred from the radiator to the cooling airflow through it. And anyone who has ever done any food canning knows that to raise the temperature of the food being canned you need to heat it in a pressure cooker. That's just what the radiator cap is used for. It does the same job as the lid on the pressure cooker. It raises the temperature of the antifreeze mix by pressurizing the cooling system from between 13 to 16 pounds per square inch. The pressure cap also seals the system so that air bubbles cannot leak into it. Thus, the pressurized and sealed cooling system transfers heat very efficiently from the engine.

The pressure cap also does double duty as the pressure relief valve for the cooling system. Any excessive overpressure of the cooling system causes the pressure relief valve of the cap to lift off its seat in the filler neck of the radiator, uncovering the opening into the overflow tube. Passage of the hot, overpressurized coolant into the overflow tank causes the coolant to expand and reduce in pressure. When the pressure of the cooling system drops to the pressure rating of the radiator cap, the pressure relief valve closes, sealing the system again.

Check the condition of the radiator cap every 12 months. Clean the seals at this time. If the seals are cracked or hardened, replace the cap. You can have the cap tested for pressure capacity by having the spring tested at a service station. Replace a cap with a weak spring.

Remember to work on the cooling system with the engine off and cooled down.

Water Pump

Engine coolant is circulated through the cooling system by the water pump, more appropriately called the coolant pump. The water pump is a centrifugal pump (Fig. 12-3). Engine coolant flows into the center or eye of the impeller of the pump. It travels along the ever-widening vanes of the impeller, where its energy or head is changed from velocity

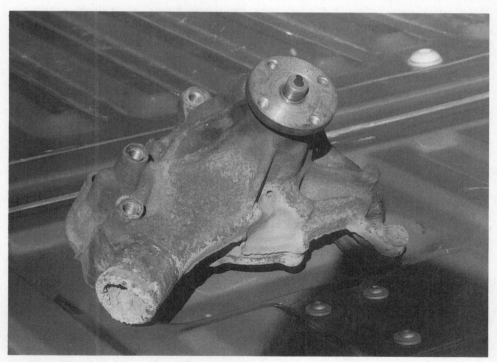

Fig. 12-3. Water pump.

energy to pressure energy. The centrifugal force at the tips of the impeller flings the coolant out of the pump and into the cylinder block.

When the engine is cold the thermostat is closed, causing flow from the engine block to recirculate through the water pump rather than flowing to the radiator. This helps the coolant to warm up quickly and prevents unnecessary cooling of the engine when it's cold, typically at start-up. Cold engines are very inefficient. When the engine warms to a preset temperature, the thermostat opens, allowing hot coolant to flow through the radiator for cooling. The cooled liquid then flows from the outlet of the radiator to the inlet of the water pump for another cycle through the engine.

Water pumps are fairly simple creatures. There is not a whole lot you can do to lengthen the life of a water pump. Be sure the coolant is kept clean and fresh. Abrasive dirt can cause premature failure of the internal seals with subsequent bearing failure of the pump. Assure that the coolant is fresh, because its anticorrosion additives protect the water pump. Maintain the V-belt that drives the pump at the specified tension. A V-belt that is adjusted too tight will cause premature pump bearing failure. A loose or worn V-belt will cause slipping and will not drive the water pump fast enough—which may, in turn, cause the engine to overheat. If the pump is driven by two belts, replace both at the same time even if only one is worn or cracked. If only one belt is replaced, all the force is put on the new belt and it will wear rapidly. When both belts are replaced, each will carry half the force. Check belt tension every month.

A water pump that is noisy or rattles is on its last leg. The bearings are worn and loose, which causes the noise. Also, any noticeable leakage of coolant—beyond a few drops through the weep hole in the bottom of the water pump—can point to internal seal failure. Either of these conditions is reason to replace the water pump.

Fans

The purpose of the fan is to pull cooling air through the radiator core. It has little, if any, direct cooling effect on the engine by itself. At idle and slow speeds the fan aids in the cooling effect of the radiator. At speeds above 35 to 40 mph, the air flowing through the radiator caused by the motion of the car provides all the cool air that is needed.

All engine fans have from four to eight blades. The blades are made of metal or plastic, and unless damaged by road debris, are maintenance-free. Sometimes the blades are spaced unevenly around the hub in an effort to reduce fan noise. Another way to reduce noise and to save on engine power is to use flexible blade fans. The pitch or twist of this type of blade changes as the speed of the fan increases. This results in each blade taking a smaller "bite" of air per revolution, saving engine power and reducing noise.

There are three types of radiator fans: direct drive, clutch type, and electric. Most engines use fans of either direct drive or clutch drive. They are mounted on the water pump shaft and receive their motive force from the V-belt and pulley arrangement that powers the water pump. Direct-drive fans can have either rigid or flexible blades.

Clutch-drive fans are usually used on cars equipped with air conditioning. The clutch-drive fan is driven only when it is needed to keep the engine from overheating, thereby reducing noise and saving engine power. When the temperature of the air flowing through the radiator core rises, the heat causes a clutch mechanism mounted at the front of the fan to gradually engage the fan to the water pump shaft. When the air temperature becomes cooler, the clutch mechanism disengages the fan from the water pump shaft, and causes the fan to coast. Clutch fans can also have either rigid or flexible blades.

Electric fans are used on cars with transverse-mounted engines and on some engines with radiators offset to one side. Electric fans are powered by an electric motor that is controlled by a thermostatic switch. The switch turns the fan on only when additional cooling air is needed and turns the fan off if sufficient air flow through the radiator exists, in order to reduce noise and save engine power. Electric fans have rigid blades only.

Most modern cars have a shroud mounted around the fan. It is not a safety device and should not be counted upon to prevent a loose fan blade from causing damage or injury if it flies off the hub. The shroud is there to improve fan performance by acting like a wind tunnel. All air pulled by the fan must pass through the radiator core, because the shroud prevents it from going anywhere else. Thus, an increase in efficiency of the fan is realized.

Keeping the fan blades, the shroud, and the clutch face (if so equipped) clean is all you can do to maintain the fan. No periodic maintenance of the clutch mechanism on clutch drive fans is recommended. Fan blades that are cracked or bent are a serious safety hazard. Replace them as soon as possible. Inspect the fan every month for damage and only with the engine off.

Thermostat

As stated above, the thermostat controls the direction of coolant flow, whether through the radiator and engine block or through the block only, depending on coolant temperature. The thermostat is a temperature-controlled valve placed between the cylinder head and the top inlet of the radiator (Fig. 12-4). As the temperature of the coolant rises, tiny copper-impregnated wax pellets inside the thermostat housing begin to melt and expand. As they expand they begin forcing a piston rod out of the thermostat housing, gradually lowering a valve and allowing more and more coolant flow to the radiator. When all the

Fig. 12-4. Thermostat.

pellets are melted, the valve is fully opened and almost all coolant flow is to the radiator via the upper inlet radiator hose. In this open position, heat can be removed from the engine by way of increased flow to the radiator.

At start-up, engine heat should be conserved as much as possible to allow the engine to warm up quickly. This reduces the build-up of moisture, sludge, and acids. In addition, higher engine temperatures improve engine efficiency. The thermostat is normally closed at start-up.

Thermostats are sold in different temperature ranges. The temperature rating of the thermostat is the temperature it is designed to open at, allowing flow of the coolant to the radiator. Most common ratings are 180, 195 and 205 degrees Fahrenheit. Thermostats are fully open at about 20 degrees Fahrenheit above these temperatures. For example, for the 180-degree thermostat, it is fully open at 200-degrees. The shop manual or owner's manual will tell you what temperature range of thermostat to use. Modern cars have thermostats for year-round use. No changing to a hot thermostat in winter and a cooler one in summer is needed or recommended.

Thermostats normally last for years. No periodic maintenance is necessary. Overheating and corrosion are enemies of thermostats. Checking the condition of the thermostat every year can help to avoid future problems. Your shop manual will tell you how to perform tests that reveal thermostat condition. Also, keeping the antifreeze fresh helps to prolong thermostat life by providing potent anticorrosion additives.

If the car overheats, takes forever to warm up, or if the passenger compartment heater does not warm up, the thermostat might be malfunctioning. Check the thermostat according to the tests in the shop manual. If it is defective, throw it away. Thermostats can't be repaired. Replace it with the correct temperature range thermostat recommended for your car.

Water Jacket

We've alluded to the water jacket of the engine in the above discussion without really defining it. Water jackets are molded into the cylinder block and cylinder head during the foundry casting process. They are merely open or hollow spaces between the outer walls of the cylinders, the inside of the cylinder block, and throughout the cylinder head. They are designed to keep the cylinders cool by providing space for the engine coolant to flow through. Keeping the antifreeze fresh will help prevent corrosion in the water jacket (Fig. 12-5).

Antifreeze

Antifreeze is the substance that makes the engine run cool. Years ago, tap water with a rust preventive additive was used as the engine coolant for most engines. This created a problem in cold weather, however, because it had to be drained to prevent freezing. To prevent water from freezing and subsequent engine or radiator damage, antifreeze is mixed with the water in all modern cars.

Antifreeze is an alcohol-based liquid called ethylene glycol. Its heat transfer characteristics are only slightly different from those of water. It is normally mixed half and half with water and recommended for year-round use. In addition, it is formulated with rust inhibitor additives to prevent rust and corrosion, and foam inhibitors to reduce

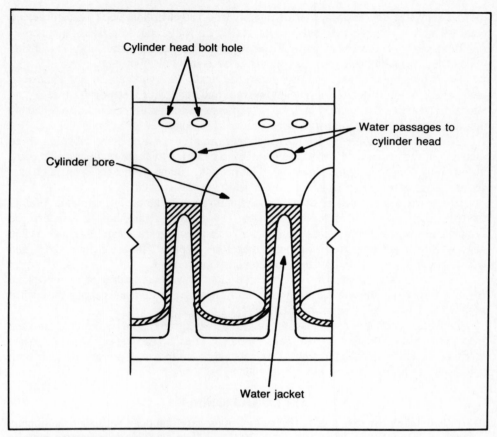

Fig. 12-5. Engine water jacket.

air entrapment and foaming since air does not conduct heat as well as the liquid coolant. Also, a red, green, or yellow dye is added to serve as a leak detector. Some antifreeze formulations contain tiny plastic beads or inorganic fibers that plug small leaks in the cooling system.

Here are a few do's and don't's in regard to antifreeze. First, never add only plain water to the cooling system. The antifreeze can become so diluted that it will boil long before it should. Temperature indicator lights are calibrated to function for properly mixed antifreeze solutions only. The temperature indicator light will not come on until well above the boiling point of water. The engine can be overheating on a weak antifreeze mixture and you wouldn't be aware of it before engine damage occurs.

If your engine or cooling system has aluminum parts, add only antifreeze that is formulated for compatibility with this metal. Not all commercial antifreeze is safe for use with aluminum.

As stated earlier, use a 50/50 mix of water and antifreeze in the cooling system and change it every 12,000 miles. A 50/50 mix freezes at −34 degrees Fahrenheit and boils at 266 degrees Fahrenheit, which is adequate for most climates. In extreme cold weather, a 64% concentration of antifreeze will lower the freezing point of the mixture to −84 degrees. Don't add antifreeze beyond 64% concentration, because the freezing point will start to rise again to only −9 degrees for a 100% concentration of antifreeze.

Keep the same mixture of water and antifreeze in the engine year-round. The engine needs the corrosion protection all year long, even in sunny Florida.

Don't mix any additives with the antifreeze mixture. If you suspect the antifreeze to be weak, flush it out of the cooling system and refill with fresh 50/50 mix. Weak antifreeze will look tan or rust in color. If you change the antifreeze mixture following our recommendation, you should never get to that point.

Years ago, water pumps had bearings that required a water pump lubricant to be mixed with the coolant. Modern cars use sealed bearings to support the impeller shaft in the pump. These bearings never need lubrication. Unless your shop manual directs the use of a water pump lubricant, *don't,* add it to the coolant.

Never use a methanol- or ethanol-based antifreeze in the cooling system. A 50/50 mixture of methanol and water boils at only 180 degrees Fahrenheit long before the temperature warning light comes on. Normal coolant temperature can be as high as 250 degrees Fahrenheit or more. You must, therefore, use the 50/50 ethylene glycol and water mix in a pressurized system for complete protection.

Test the antifreeze mixture every three months with an antifreeze tester. If the tester indicates that the antifreeze is weak, better flush the system and replace the coolant with a fresh mixture as soon as practical.

Perform a complete cooling system check according to the instructions in the shop manual every 25,000 miles or two years. In the fall of each year inspect for leaks. When working around the cooling system, remember that antifreeze is poisonous. Don't get it in your mouth or on your skin or in your eyes.

AIR CONDITIONING

More than half of the cars sold in the United States are equipped with air conditioning. Typical cooling or refrigeration capacity is 20,000 BTU/hour. This refrigeration capacity allows the passenger compartment temperature to be lowered by 25 to 30 degrees Fahrenheit with the car moving at 30 mph. Air conditioning is another heat transfer process similar, although more complicated, than the cooling system heat transfer process.

Theory

In a passenger car air conditioning system, the working fluid is usually Freon-12 (Fig. 12-6). The Freon-12 flows through a radiator-like device called an evaporator. As it does so, it picks up heat from the hot air flowing across the evaporator inside the car. As the Freon-12 heats up it vaporizes to a gas and flows to a belt-driven, clutch-activated compressor. The compressor pressurizes the gas, causing its temperature to rise.

From the compressor, the hot, pressurized Freon-12 gas flows to another radiator-like device called a condenser. The condenser is usually mounted in front of the engine radiator. In the condenser, the Freon-12 gas loses heat to the cool air flowing through the condenser fins and condenses back into a liquid. The liquid Freon-12 then flows to a storage tank, sometimes called a dryer. Any water in the Freon-12 is removed by the dryer to prevent formation of corrosive hydrochloric acid.

The Freon-12 flows next to the expansion valve. In the expansion valve the Freon-12 is expanded from a relatively cool, high-pressure liquid to a much colder, low-pressure

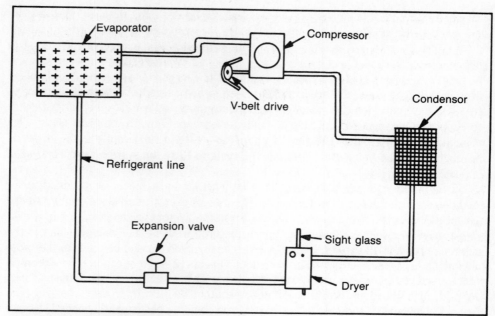

Fig. 12-6. Air conditioning system.

gas. This process (actually boiling of the Freon-12) requires heat to work. The heat is supplied by the hot air from inside the car passenger compartment. As the Freon-12 absorbs heat, it cools the fins in the evaporator, allowing the hot air from the car to transfer its heat to the fins. Cooled air flows back into the passenger compartment, and the cycle starts over again.

In addition to cooling the passenger compartment air, the air conditioning system will also dehumidify the air. This is done as water vapor in the humid air condenses inside the evaporator and is drained beneath the car. Sometimes a small puddle of water forms under the car from this drainage. This is a normal occurrence. In very humid air this condensed moisture might freeze and block the cooling fins of the evaporator. To prevent this, the suction throttling value (shown in Fig. 12-6) keeps the condensed water vapor out of the evaporator by pulling it back into the low pressure line, where it will eventually be removed from the system by the dryer.

Most air conditioning systems in modern cars are combined with the heating, defrosting, and ventilating systems. These systems normally share common ductwork. Thus, the proper type of air (heated, air conditioned, etc.) is directed through the ductwork, depending on the setting of the mode switch on the control panel. The air is directed by flapper doors that direct the proper amount of air through the ductwork to the appropriate outlet vents inside the car. Your shop manual will locate these doors and explain their operation.

Problems

The day you need the air conditioning the most could be the day it lets you down. Air conditioning problems can usually be traced to low refrigerant level, a loose compressor drive belt, a blown fuse or relay, a system leak, or flapper door troubles. Besides the compressor, the controls and flapper doors are the only moving parts of the system.

A sight glass is used in some systems to determine the amount of refrigerant in the system. If the glass is clear it indicates either a fully charged or empty system. If the system provides cool air, you can assume it is charged. If you see a few bubbles through the sight glass, the system might need to be charged. A foamy appearance in the sight glass indicates the system is just about empty and needs to be fully charged. Be especially alarmed if you notice a cloudy appearance through the sight glass. This most likely indicates that the drying chemical—called a dessicant—in the dryer is disintegrating and is being drawn through the system. Have the system serviced as soon as possible.

If the system needs a charge, have it serviced by a mechanic certified in air conditioning. You can buy a do-it-yourself recharge kit from an auto store, but we advise against this. Low refrigerant levels usually mean the system has a leak. To find a leak, a repairman uses a specially designed propane torch whose flame changes color in the presence of Freon-12 vapors. Fixing leaks, is an involved service best left to the pros, but finding leaks can be just plain hazardous. Freon-12 (or any other type Freon) is transformed into phosgene gas by the torch flame. This is commonly called mustard gas, and is deadly. Handling the Freon-12 poses another danger: if, while recharging, the Freon-12 blows back and gets in your eyes, you could be permanently blinded. Do *not* attempt this type of service yourself.

You can check the operation of the compressor and its clutch very simply. Start the car with the air conditioner off. Have someone turn the air conditioning on as you watch the clutch on the compressor. If the clutch does not engage, service is needed.

Preventive Maintenance

Run the air conditioner a few minutes every month both summer and winter. This causes the Freon-12 refrigerant to circulate throughout the system and helps keep all the seals in the various components lubricated. Lubricated seals won't crack or dry out, and will help prevent refrigerant loss.

Check the condition of and adjust the compressor V-belt every month. Replace cracked, glazed, or frayed belts. Adjust the belt with a tension gauge according to factory specifications.

Check the level and condition of the refrigerant every month. If your system doesn't have a sight glass check the system pressure instead at the low-pressure side port. Consult the shop manual for pressure readings that indicate whether recharging is necessary.

Clean the outside of the condenser in much the same manner you clean the engine radiator. Remove bugs and other debris from between the condenser fins, being careful not to bend any of the fins. Straighten them if they are bent. Clean the condenser monthly.

Check the operation of the flapper doors twice a year. Make sure all the controls are working properly at this time by checking the connection of all vacuum lines to the controls.

Test and tune up the system every two years, yearly if you live in a hot climate. Remember that most repairs should be left to a certified air conditioning mechanic. If you live in a colder climate, consider removing the compressor drive belt in the winter if it doesn't operate other equipment. Even with the air conditioning load off the belt, the belt will turn the compressor clutch, resulting in a slight loss of engine efficiency.

SUMMARY OF RECOMMENDATIONS

- Inspect and clean the cooling system radiator monthly.
- Flush the cooling system every 12,000 miles and refill with fresh antifreeze mix. Test the coolant every three months with an antifreeze tester.
- Check the coolant level weekly. Check for signs of scum or sediment in the overflow tank.
- Check the radiator cap every 12 months. Consider replacing the cap every 100,000 miles regardless of condition.
- Check the water pump V-belt condition and tension monthly.
- Inspect the fan blades monthly for cracks or bending.
- Don't add rust inhibitor to antifreeze. Certain types may contaminate the antifreeze mix by reacting adversely with antirust compounds already in the antifreeze.
- Never use a methanol or ethanol based antifreeze.
- Run the air conditioner a few minutes every month year-round to keep seals lubricated.
- Check monthly the condition and tension of the air conditioning compressor V-belt, the refrigerant level, and clean the condenser.
- Check the operation of the air conditioning flapper doors and controls twice a year.

MECHANIC'S TIPS

- When replacing cooling system drive belts, consider replacing all the belts at the same time. Chances are they are all worn.
- Never remove a thermostat to prevent engine overheating. Find the cause of the overheating condition and solve it. Use a new gasket when replacing the thermostat.
- Never add plain water to the cooling system. Use only the proper water/antifreeze mix year-round.
- Leave air conditioning system charging to your mechanic.
- Consider removing the air conditioning compressor belt in the winter to increase gas mileage.

13

When Trouble Strikes

EVERYTHING THAT MANKIND DOES OR MAKES WILL EVENTUALLY HAVE OR DEVELOP TROU-
ble. A loose interpretation of the Second Law of Thermodynamics states: All natural
processes, without input of work, tend to a state of greater disorder. Unless you
periodically unclutter your desk, it will eventually look like a trash heap. Unless you
periodically maintain your house, it will eventually crumble. And unless you properly
maintain your car, it will eventually break down or rust away to a sorry, brown powder.

No one, anywhere, anyhow, can keep a car factory-fresh throughout the years. Your
car will gradually wear out. Of course, the whole purpose of this book is to slow down
that wearing-out process by offering sound advice on preventive maintenance. Even with
the best of care, things will sometimes go wrong. Car designers build warning systems
into our cars to forewarn us of imminent trouble. We can also learn to recognize trouble
by using our senses when warning systems don't exist.

We can use our senses of smell, hearing, sight, and touch to help us in the absence
of warning lights, buzzers, or gauges. For example, do you smell the odor of brake fluid? Perhaps the master cylinder is leaking. Hear a rumbling noise under the car? Perhaps the muffler is shot. Do you see steam blowing out of the engine compartment?
Maybe the car is overheating. Do the tires feel hot? Maybe the brakes need adjustment.
The point is, when trouble strikes, you can't always rely on the dashboard idiot lights
to warn you. In fact, when an idiot light flashes on, damage may already be done. You
need to recognize trouble before it gets a death grip on your car. In this chapter, we
will cover some of the ways to spot trouble in the early stages. First let's cover the
standard instrumentation found on most cars.

WARNING LIGHTS AND ALARMS

Oil Pressure

Most cars come equipped with an indicator light that signals the driver when the oil pressure in the engine lubrication system is low. Some cars are equipped with gauges that indicate the oil pressure in pounds per square inch (psi). In either case, the oil pressure is sensed by a device that is screwed into the engine block in the area of an oil passage. The sensor has a spring-loaded diaphragm that pushes a slider along a resistance as oil pressure changes (Fig. 13-1). As the resistance changes, so does the needle in the gauge that you read inside the car. If the diaphragm does not bend to move the slider, either the oil pressure is low or zero, or the engine is off. With the engine off and the key in the ignition, the oil gauge will read zero or the low oil pressure light will come on. This is normal. If the light doesn't come on, replace the bulb.

With the engine running, a low oil pressure indication normally means there is insufficient oil pressure available to move the oil through the various passages in the engine block. This can be a result of low oil level or failure of the oil pump, both of which can very quickly lead to loss of lubrication of vital engine parts such as bearings and cylinders. Serious damage can result from continued engine operation at low oil pressure. The car should be pulled off the road immediately upon low oil pressure indication and the engine shut off. Have the car towed to a garage to investigate the problem.

If your car is equipped with an oil pressure warning light only, consider installing an oil pressure gauge in addition to the light. Oil pressure gauges allow you to see trouble coming before it's too late. With a gauge you can see the pressure dropping off from normal and pull off the road before oil pressure is dangerously low. With only a warning light, you have no idea whether you are losing pressure until it's too late. Warning lights

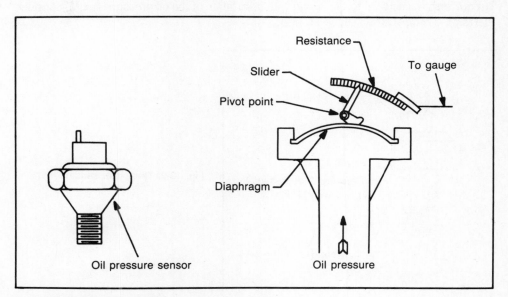

Fig. 13-1. Oil pressure sensor.

are set to indicate low oil pressure at far too low a value to avoid damage. If the oil pressure drops gradually over a few days, suspect an oil leak. A sudden drop in oil pressure could point to a blown gasket or failed oil pump.

Don't fool around with low oil pressure readings. Investigate and solve oil pressure problems immediately. Failure to do so could ruin the whole engine.

Engine Temperature

Your car will tell you when things are getting a little too hot under the hood with another warning device called the temperature sending unit and warning light or temperature gauge.

The temperature measured is the coolant temperature. When the coolant gets too hot, it means more heat is being transferred to the coolant from the engine than the coolant can dissipate or retransfer through the radiator to the outside air. This could indicate a coolant loss, a blocked or closed thermostat, or that the engine is running hot from lubricant loss, for instance.

The coolant temperature is measured by a thermistor sending unit located in the water jacket of the engine block. As coolant temperature rises, the electrical resistance of the thermistor decreases. This results in an increase of current to the temperature gauge. The pointer on the gauge rises or falls in proportion to the electrical resistance of the thermistor sending unit (Fig. 13-2).

A warning light will only signal high or low engine temperature; it won't tell you anything else. A gauge can alert you to a potential problem long before it gets to the emergency stage. If, for example, you notice a gradual rise in operating temperature over a few days, suspect that the coolant level is dropping. Erratic temperature readings could indicate a faulty thermostat. You can predict these kinds of things with gauges, but not with warning lights. So, along with installation of the oil pressure gauge, consider installing a temperature gauge as well.

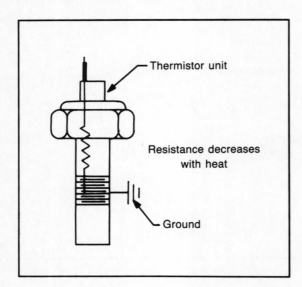

Fig. 13-2. Thermistor sending unit.

Thermistor unit

Resistance decreases with heat

Ground

Alternator/Generator/Battery

The third gauge usually included in the instrument panel is the alternator/generator/battery gauge. It may be labeled "ammeter gauge" or just "generator gauge." The ammeter provides information on the electrical charging system. It, therefore, is connected to the alternator/generator, the battery, and the voltage regulator. It tells you whether the battery is receiving a charge from the alternator/generator (charging) or losing electricity to the charging circuit (discharging).

The ammeter is wired into the circuit between the alternator/generator and the battery. It measures the amount of current flow and the direction of that flow between the alternator/generator and the battery. When current flows into the battery from the alternator/generator it is called a charging condition. The current flows through a small coil of wire inside the ammeter, inducing a magnetic field in the coil which pulls on a small magnet attached to the gauge needle. This causes the needle to pivot to the right of center, or the plus side of the gauge scale. If the current reverses—flowing from the battery to the alternator/generator—it is called a discharging condition. The reversed flow of current causes the needle to pivot to the opposite (left) or minus side of the gauge. Under normal conditions, the needle will rest just slightly into the positive side of the gauge scale. It is normal for the needle to move slightly around the center point between plus and minus (Fig. 13-3).

If the needle gradually moves toward the minus side while you are driving, the battery is discharging. You must take action quickly or the battery will soon be dead. In this case, don't stop the car; you might not be able to start it again. Instead, switch off all unnecessary electrical equipment (air conditioning, heater, radio, etc.) and head for the nearest service station. If the station is no more than a few miles away you should be able to make it.

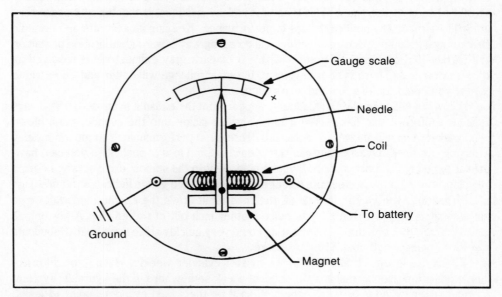

Fig. 13-3. Ammeter.

If your car is not equipped with an ammeter gauge, it will have an on-off type warning light that activates when the battery is discharging. The light should always activate at start-up. If it doesn't, replace the bulb. Consider installing an ammeter gauge or voltmeter gauge for better charging system indication. The ammeter can forewarn you of impending electrical problems, whereas a simple warning light cannot.

SIGNS, SOUNDS, AND ODORS

Reading gauges and being on the alert for warning lights are not the only ways to detect potential car troubles. You need to use all your senses as feedback for signs of trouble. Things that smell or seem unusual are just as important an indication as the warnings (maybe more so) that lights and gauges offer.

Fuel, Brake Fluid, and Antifreeze

Every driver recognizes the smell of gasoline. There's nothing else that smells quite like it. It's normal to smell gasoline shortly after refueling. A few drops will always spill down the side of the car or the fumes may enter through an open window and linger inside the passenger compartment. If you smell gasoline long after refueling or suddenly while driving, it could indicate a fuel leak. Stop the car immediately. Check for leaks around the carburetor, the engine compartment fuel lines, and the gas tank and filler tube and hose. Gasoline leaks are nothing to procrastinate over; get them fixed fast.

Another sign of trouble is black or very dark gray exhaust fumes. This is a sign of carburetion or ignition problems. Black or dark gray smoke from the exhaust pipe is actually unburned or partially burned gasoline. It could indicate an improper air-fuel mixture setting on the carburetor, a defective carburetor, or spark plug malfunction. If the spark plugs are in good shape, perhaps the ignition wiring or distributor assembly need service or replacement. This type of trouble is insidious, in that it might occur very gradually without any noticeable loss in performance. Keeping an accurate and periodic check on gas mileage, perhaps monthly, will go a long way toward identification of ignition and carburetion problems. If you notice black or dark gray exhaust get it resolved as soon as practical. There is no emergency, but your mileage will suffer and, in extreme cases, you could foul the oil and spark plugs.

Billows of white smoke that suddenly appear from the exhaust system almost always indicate antifreeze that has leaked from the water jacket into the cylinder via a blown head gasket. You will also notice a marked decrease in performance. You must not delay in having this fixed. Overheating can result quickly from loss of coolant. If you can, have the car towed to a service station. If you must drive it to the station, drive slowly, keeping a vigilant watch on the temperature gauge. The instant the gauge indicates the first sign of overheating, you've had it. Pull off the road, shut down the engine, and wait or go for assistance on foot. Don't try to coax another inch out of the engine. A hot engine is bad enough, but one that is overheating could very quickly seize from heat. Rebuilding a seized engine could cost $1000 or more.

Check the level of brake fluid in the master cylinder weekly. Having to add brake fluid more often than normal is a sure sign of a leak somewhere in the hydraulic system. A wet master cylinder or wet connection to it or the wheel cylinders point to leaks. Sometimes a leak can find its way inside the car and collect on the brake pedal or drip underneath it. For safety's sake have the brake system serviced immediately at the first sign of a leak.

Oil

Oil leaks are rare on modern cars. If you have an oil leak, the area under suspicion will look wet compared to the dry, sometimes dusty, look of a normal engine. If the wet area is around the oil filler cap, perhaps all that is needed is for you to be more careful of spills next time you add oil. In any case, wipe the area clean and dry. Check it again after operating the car for a short time. If it's wet again in the same area, the engine is leaking oil. If it's dry, perhaps it was originally due to a spill or road splash. Check oil level to be safe.

Light gray smoke exiting from the exhaust system is a sure sign of oil burning. It's not much fun, as you know, following someone whose car is burning oil. If it's your car burning oil, get it fixed. It's a nuisance to other drivers, and is an air pollutant. Most likely the piston rings are starting to wear, allowing oil to flow past the piston into the combustion chamber where the oil is burned during the ignition stroke. If you suspect oil burning, check your oil level every few days or so. A gradually depleting level of oil combined with the light gray exhaust smoke points to oil burning.

Noise

You spend more time in your car than anyone else. You should know all of its little idiosyncrasies. A mechanic can't tell whether a noise he hears is normal for your car or is sounding out trouble. Only you can do that.

Noises can be divided into those that occur as the car is moving and those that occur with the car at idle or parked with the engine running. If the noise occurs only while the car is moving, it is most likely caused by a problem with the chassis, suspension, or transmission. If the noise occurs while the car is at idle, it probably is coming from the engine or accessory equipment.

Explaining to someone else how a noise sounds and where it is coming from is a little like trying to tell the doctor where the pain is and how much it hurts. Table 13-1 will give you some general information regarding sound analysis on your car.

ORGANIZATIONS

If you belong to an auto club, you will always have a friend when you need help. Most of the larger and better clubs have offices and contract service stations nationwide. There are a few who have branched into Canada, Mexico, and beyond.

Their basic promise is that in return for an annual membership fee they guarantee certain kinds and extents of emergency assistance when and where you need it. There is usually a free magazine subscription and a number of other benefits included in membership. Even if you do not travel extensively, it's still a good deal to join a club. Dues are modest, ranging from $15 to $50 or so. Table 13-2 lists services and benefits available from most clubs and divides them into three categories: necessary, desirable, and nonessential. Choose a club that offers, at least, those benefits and services listed as necessary and desirable.

Table 13-1. Troubling Sounds and Their Causes.

Sound	Check
A loud bang from exhaust or intake manifolds	Ignition timing, air-fuel mixture, valves
A steady tapping sound from engine	Valves
A steady clicking sound from wheels	Wheel bearings, hub caps, wheel nuts
A steady clicking sound from engine	Valve lifter
A grinding or growling sound from wheels	Wheel bearings
A grinding or growling sound from differential	Differential, axle shaft bearings
A knock or ping from engine	Timing, spark plugs, octane level of fuel
A thud or thump under car	Exhaust system
A high-pitched whine from engine	Timing gear, distributer drive, oil pump drive
A whistling sound from wheels	Power steering drive belt
A short put-put sound from tailpipe	Exhaust valves, air fuel mixture
A dull thumping sound from under car	U-joints
A squeak or scraping sound from wheels	Brake pads or linings
A high-pitched, shrill sound from engine	V-belts

SPARE PARTS

Owners who take pride in their cars will want to keep small supplies of parts on hand in order to cut down on wasteful emergency trips to the auto store or dealer. Collect the parts as they go on sale at the auto store. Stores usually include flyers with the Sunday newspaper advertising upcoming sales. You will save money and time and will be satisfied knowing the spares are readily available on the shelf in your basement or garage.

What sort of spare parts are we talking about? Well, they can be divided into those carried along on long trips and those that normally remain at home. See Tables 13-3 and 13-4 for some ideas. If you are planning to keep your car for a long time, stock up on parts. If you don't use them, they will add resale value to the car when you include them in a future sale.

EMERGENCY TOOL SETS

Along with the parts kit for long trips, carry an emergency tool set. In fact, it's a good idea to carry the tool set in the car at all times. Don't go overboard by packing a myriad

Table 13-2. Auto Club Services.

Service or Benefit	Necessary	Desirable	Nonessential
Emergency road service	X		
Travel service maps, insurance, etc.		X	
Road condition information service		X	
Hotel reservation service			X
Accident insurance benefits			X
Car theft insurance benefits			X
Notory public service			X
License and title service			X
Car rental discount service		X	
Bail bond service		X	
International driving permit service			X
Toll-free emergency number	X		
Travelers check service			X
Emergency check cashing service		X	
Passport Photo service			X
Emergency lock and key service	X		
Towing service	X		
Legal defense service			X

Table 13-3. Spare Parts for a Long Trip.

1. 1 Quart of oil
2. Fan belt or belts
3. Spare headlight
4. Spare bulb for brake light and turn signal light
5. Spare fuses
6. 1 spare spark plug
7. Can WD-40
8. Battery water
9. Spare hose
10. Carburetor cleaner
11. Antifreeze mixture

Table 13-4. Spare Parts to Keep on Hand at Home.

1. Case of oil	16. Windshield washer fluid
2. Oil filters	17. Brake fluid
3. Grease	18. Power steering fluid
4. WD-40	(if equipped with power steering)
5. Silicone lubricant	19. Cleaners, waxes
6. White grease	20. Bucket, sponges, rags, brushes, chamois
7. Graphite lubricant	21. 1 Gallon of antifreeze
8. Set of spark plugs	22. Tire stem caps
9. Air filter element	23. Carburetor cleaner
10. Fuel filter element	24. Dry gas
11. Spare fuses	25. Spare distributor cap and rotor
12. Spare head light	26. Cotter pins
13. Spare bulbs for all interior/exterior lighting	27. Touch-up paint
14. Spare fan belt(s)	28. Spare PCV valve
15. Battery water	29. Heater hose, radiator hose, vacuum hose

of tools, meters, and gauges into your car. They take up space and, really, only a few important ones are necessary. If you don't feel like assembling the set yourself, you can buy sets fitted in compact and attractive carrying cases at auto stores and from mail-order houses.

If you assemble your own set, you can buy tools of less-than-premium quality as long as they are safe. Remember, they are for emergency use only. If they get used only a few times over the life of the car and hold up, that's all you should ask of them. If you find the need for them more than that, you probably need to spruce up your preventive maintenance activities, or the car might need major repairs. Whether you assemble the set yourself or buy it, it should include, as a minimum, the items listed in Table 13-5.

SUMMARY OF RECOMMENDATIONS

■ Where possible and practical, install gauges in place of, or in concert with, warning lights. Typical applications are an oil pressure gauge, a temperature gauge, and an ammeter or voltmeter.

■ Pull off the road and shut the engine down immediately if low oil pressure or engine overheating is indicated.

■ Consider joining one of the better national auto clubs.

■ Learn to recognize signs of potential problems through interpretation of instrument panel readings.

■ Learn to apply your senses of sight, sound, touch, and smell as your personal information-gathering network for recognizing potential problems.

MECHANIC'S TIPS

■ Carry an emergency road kit in the car at all times. It should consist of the following as a minimum: road flares and/or reflectors, a list of emergency telephone numbers, $10 in cash plus coins for emergency telephone calls, 1 quart of oil, gasoline hand pump, first aid kit.

Table 13-5. Emergency Tool Set.

1. Jumper cables—at least 8 feet long and 11 gauge
2. Tire pressure gauge
3. Fuse puller
4. Jackknife
5. 2 screwdrivers—Phillips and flat
6. Slip joint pliers
7. Rubber mallet
8. Open end wrenches (to fit the majority of fasteners)
9. Hose clamps
10. Gloves and coveralls
11. Flashlight and spare batteries
12. Emergency flasher or flares
13. A scrap of copper wire (to tie up a loose muffler or tailpipe)
14. Spare blanket or sportsmans blanket
15. Lug wrench
16. Distress flag or marker
17. Ice scraper and brush
18. Siphon
19. First aid kit
20. 1 can of aerosol flat fix
21. Rags and hand cleaner

■ When making emergency road calls, hang up the telephone last. Make sure the emergency road service or police have all the details before you hang up. Some details to report are: your location, name, license plate number, type of car, suspected problem, number of people in your party, and any injuries—if in an accident.

14

Year-Round Driving Tips

YOUR CAR MIGHT LAST 250 YEARS IF YOU NEVER DRIVE IT. IT MIGHT LAST 50 YEARS IF YOU drive it only to church on Sunday. And it might last only 2 years if you drive it every day like a maniac, regardless of the preventive maintenance you perform.

You must realize that your car is constructed of hundreds of parts that are bolted, screwed, and welded together. You need to be aware that there are dozens of fine adjustments that must be made and maintained throughout the car to keep it running smoothly. Poor driving habits and reckless driving tend to undo your car. Soon, joints loosen up and adjustments need to be attended to. Make every effort to break poor driving habits. Drive like your life and your car's life depend on it, because they do. By following the driving tips outlined below, you should be able to add many miles of life to your car, and keep some of those hard-earned dollars in your wallet.

SPRING, SUMMER, AND FALL
Engine

1. Avoid sudden stops and starts; easy does it.
2. Avoid revving the engine.
3. Take your time wherever you go. If you get to where you're going early, you'll only have to wait.
4. Shut the engine off if the car is idling more than a few minutes. You're wasting gas otherwise.
5. Check oil, coolant, battery, and power steering fluid levels periodically as recommended in earlier chapters. Do it every 500 miles on a cross-country trip.

Transmission

1. Check transmission fluid level before taking a long trip.
2. Make sure the car is completely stopped before shifting from forward to reverse or reverse to forward; don't be in a rush.
3. Don't spin the wheels on slippery surfaces or loose stones. When they suddenly grab solid road they will put a tremendous torque on the drivetrain.
4. Don't pop the clutch or "wind" the car out in any one gear; your high school days are over!

Tires

1. Keep sudden stops and starts at a minimum, for emergencies only.
2. Keep tires properly inflated at all times.
3. Slow down for corners and curves.
4. Drive around glass, metal, or potholes in or on the road.
5. Take bumps in the road lightly. Drive slowly over railroad tracks.

Brakes and Suspension

1. Apply brakes gradually and firmly. Avoid slamming them on.
2. Don't "ride" the brakes while driving.
3. Take your foot off the brake for just a second to cool them off, such as when traveling down a long, steep hill.
4. Drive as evenly and as smoothly as possible under all road conditions. Your springs, shocks and suspension joints will thank you.

Miscellaneous Tips

1. Park your car away from objects such as other cars, curbs, telephone poles, parking meters, and trees.
2. Keep your distance behind other vehicles, especially trucks.
3. Don't drive while drunk, angry or emotionally upset. Have someone else drive.
4. For better gas mileage, try driving at an average speed of about 45 to 50 mph where legal. Most cars get their best mileage at this speed.
5. If you're going on a trip, pack luggage wisely on car top carriers. Keep the pile well tied down, as low as possible, with taller items toward the rear. This saves on gasoline by keeping aerodynamic drag on the car to a minimum. Remove the luggage racks when you're done with them.

WINTER DRIVING

1. Don't spin the tires in ice or snow or rock the car to free it. Push it or have it towed.
2. Keep winter speeds reduced. You will still get to where you're going in time by leaving earlier.
3. Don't downshift while traveling up an icy hill. You'll lose traction and could find yourself in a real fix if there is traffic behind you.
4. Remove tire chains when regular or snow tires will provide needed traction.

5. Keep the battery fully charged at all times.
6. For extremely cold-weather operation, install an engine oil heater for easier starting. Carry a can of ether spray for emergency starting. (*Caution:* ether is poisonous.) Don't crank a cold engine more than 30 seconds at a time.
7. Make sure the heater, defroster, windshield wipers, and washers are in top shape. Carry an ice scraper, brush, and even an aerosal windshield de-icer.
8. Drive smoothly and conservatively on slick roads. Don't make sudden or jerky movements. And don't drive until the windows are clear of frost or ice.
9. Install snow tires before the first snow. Installing them over the Thanksgiving holiday usually works out well.
10. Stopping distances increase by over 400% on ice and snow. Gauge yourself accordingly. Keep the wheels pointed straight ahead when moving through deep snow. Leave the plowing to the snow plow.

Fuel Selection

Oil companies formulate their gasolines with dry gas during the winter months to help prevent moisture entrapment in the fuel system. Therefore, there are normally no special gasolines or additives to buy during the winter. Adding a can of dry gas to your tank won't hurt anything but your pocketbook.

Oil Selection

Multiviscosity oils behave like thin oils at low temperatures and like thick oils at high temperatures. If you use a 30-weight oil year-round, you might experience starting problems in the winter, especially if your battery is weak. Using a 10W-30 or 10W-40 oil will allow easier starting in the winter, because at low temperatures the oil behaves like a thinner 10-weight oil. In extremely cold climates, consider using a 5W-20 oil for good starting down to −10 degrees Fahrenheit. For even colder climates, you should be using a preheater to heat the oil overnight.

15

Putting It All Together

HOPEFULLY THE INFORMATION YOU FOUND IN THIS BOOK WILL BE THE BEGINNING OF A NEW awareness for you as you take your first steps toward improved car care. Even if your car isn't new or has been neglected in the past, following the suggestions and recommendations presented here should result in extended life for your car. Decide now to put the added time and effort necessary into your routine activities for improved car life and performance.

SCHEDULES

We mentioned the word routine in the last paragraph. That's exactly what you must develop to guarantee proper car maintenance. Establishing a routine for doing any chore always makes it less of an anguish to perform. Find the time during your busy week to spend with your car. Choose a time when no one else will bother you. Early Saturday mornings before other family members wake seems to work for many people. Set aside an hour to give your car the attention called for. Plan your activities before you start.

In Appendix C you will find service charts you can use to perform all the suggested maintenance items covered in this book. You may photocopy the charts if you desire or perhaps construct your own. In any case, stick to our suggestions and perform them faithfully.

A word of caution is in order, however. People overeat, they overdrink, overreact to situations, etc.—and you can overdo it with car maintenance. Remember, your car is there to serve you. Don't become a slave to it. Don't put off a family activity just to wash the car or perform some other routine service on it. There are a great number of more important and satisfying things in life than changing engine oil. Keep your head about you and establish priorities, and any list of priorities should include family and job before car.

Mileage

If you decide to construct your own service chart, include items that are to be serviced according to mileage. Such items include oil changes, grease jobs, and tire rotation. Mileage on a car is directly related to rubbing, sliding, and abrasive wear. It also correlates to additive depletion in oil, grease, and automatic transmission fluid. Use the mileage frequency recommendations included herein for optimum results.

Time and Frequency

Include in your chart items to be serviced at certain time intervals rather than at mileage intervals. These items include washing and waxing, checking tire pressure, etc. Time is a factor in additive depletion, dirt accumulation, acid and sludge buildup in the crankcase, etc. Use the time frequency recommendations presented herein for best results.

RECORD KEEPING

The act of keeping financial records is called accounting. The act of keeping automotive records is called good sense. Be sure to develop lots of good sense.

Keep accurate, detailed records of all service work you or your mechanic perform on your car. Record the date and mileage, who performed the service, and what was done. Save all receipts for parts and service, in addition to all warranty contracts. And stick with it. Lapses in recording of work done have a way of never getting recorded.

What's so important about record keeping? For one thing, accurate records let you know where you are in terms of your maintenance schedule. Records let you know what has been done and when, and what needs to be done and when you should do it. Records, therefore, are primarily for planning purposes.

Records are important also in diagnostic work. If you find, through a review of your records, that gas mileage has been steadily dropping off, you could deduce that it's time for a tune-up or that other repairs might be necessary. Records can also add value to your car at resale time. A prospective buyer will be greatly impressed by the detailed, historical automotive account you can show him or her. The buyer will know exactly the condition of the car, and will feel confident in knowing that there is less likelihood of surprise repairs to be made. The buyer will know what service was last performed and what comes next. A complete service record is a valuable commodity, indeed.

One last advantage in keeping good records: they add a lot of weight to your case in warranty or faulty repair disputes. If you can show documented evidence of when a repair was done, you stand a much improved chance for winning in a faulty repair argument. Keep a record of the date and mileage that a repair was done along with the service writer or manager's name and the mechanic's name, if you can get it. Also, record what was done and have any used parts returned to you. Some warranty work needs to be done only by the dealer to keep the warranty in effect. In order not to void the warranty, make sure you know which repairs you or your mechanic can legally make and those that must be handled only by the dealer.

DEALER CONTACT

Develop a friendly relationship with the dealer, especially the service manager or a mechanic. The dealer will be able to supply you with information on ordering shop manuals and any special tooling needed for your car. He will also be a source of information on service bulletins published by the manufacturer. Service bulletins advise the dealer on special items or techniques of service for the cars he sells. A friendly service manager might allow you to review or even photocopy (if allowed by the publisher or manufacturer) the service bulletins for your information and/or files.

In addition to being a source of service information, the dealer is the only person authorized to offer extended warranties for purchase. These are usually limited warranties and can cost up to $300. They are of some value, so check to see if you can purchase one for your car.

WHEN TO SELL

There are only three occasions when you should consider selling your car: after an accident for which repairs would be exorbitant in cost, when you can no longer buy parts from the dealer, or when the cost per mile to operate the car becomes too high.

If you have an accident, your car is considered a total loss if the cost to repair the car will surpass the market value of a similar car in good condition. If damages total $2,500 while the market value of your car (unwrecked) is only $2,000, the insurance company will most likely opt to replace your wrecked car with another car of equal market value. Or perhaps they will award you $2,000 and leave it to you to decide whether to repair your car or buy another one. Of course, if you decide to replace your car with a used car, you will normally have little idea how the used car has been maintained. See Appendix A for tips on buying a used car.

Whether to buy a new car, a used car, or have your car repaired is a tough decision. Buying new will cost a lot of money, but you aren't going to inherit someone else's problems as you would if buying a used car. Consider this: if your wrecked car has suffered primarily body damage, it might be worthwhile to have it repaired. Repaired bodies don't have an effect on car performance. You should still get the same mileage, oil usage, tire wear, etc. as you did before the accident. The only thing you need to be concerned with is the weatherability of the repaired body: will it leak water inside, will it be more susceptible to rusting, will it rattle or squeak, how's the rider comfort going to be? The body shop can help you answer these questions.

New car auto dealers can order new parts for your car for at least 10 years after the year of manufacture. New cars bought in 1977 should still have new parts available for them through 1987. However, after 10 years new parts inventories will rapidly deplete. For our example, starting in 1988 new car dealers are no longer required to carry new parts for 1977 cars. They might still be able to order them, but when manufacturer inventories run out, you're out of luck. At that point you must move to the next source of parts—auto stores and junkyards.

Auto stores carry a variety of new and rebuilt auto parts for older cars. New parts usually consist of spark plugs, oil/air/gas filters, batteries, hoses, belts, distributor caps, rotors, brake shoes, shocks, and radiator caps—to name a few. Rebuilt parts are typically things such as carburetors, alternators, starter motors, voltage regulators, and sometimes completely rebuilt engines. Some stores offer a trade-in allowance on old parts and even

Table 15-1. Cost of Operating the Family Car.

(Depreciation at 10% per year)

	Year 1	Year 2	Year 3	Year 4	Year 5	Year 6	Year 7	Year 8	Year 9	Year 10	Total
Depreciation	$1,000	$1,000	$1,000	$1,000	$1,000	$1,000	$1,000	$1,000	$1,000	$1,000	$10,000
Gasoline	$500	$492	$480	$480	$460	$455	$460	$460	$455	$460	$4,702
Oil	$60	$60	$60	$60	$60	$60	$60	$60	$60	$60	$600
Tires	$200	-	-	$400	$200	-	-	$400	$200	-	$1,400
Repairs	$75	$200	$250	$600	$550	$600	$600	$400	$200	$100	$3,575
Insurance	$450	$450	$450	$400	$400	$300	$300	$300	$300	$300	$3,650
License, fees, misc.	$150	$85	$85	$85	$85	$75	$75	$75	$75	$75	$865
Total cost	$2,435	$2,287	$2,325	$3,025	$2,755	$2,490	$2,495	$2,695	$2,290	$1,995	$24,792
Miles	12,000	12,000	12,000	12,000	12,000	12,000	12,000	12,000	12,000	12,000	120,000
Cost per mile	20.3¢	19.1¢	19.4¢	25.2¢	23.0¢	20.8¢	20.8¢	22.4¢	19.1¢	16.6¢	20.7¢

Note: Price of car $10,000
Assume 12,000 miles driven each year
Change oil every 2,000 miles at $10 for oil and filter = $60 per year
Snow tires purchased during years 1, 5, and 9
Regular tires purchased during years 4 and 8

guarantee rebuilt parts for a short time after installation. Deal with a reputable auto store and you'll do just fine.

Junkyards are another story, however. In most cases, when you buy a part for your car from a junkyard you will get no guarantee with it. If it doesn't work after you get the part home and installed on your car, you're out of luck. Usually, reputable junk dealers only guarantee that a part will work at the time of purchase. If it lasts just 2 miles or 1 day you have no recourse. About the only thing you can do is to have the part tested at the junkyard before you pay for it. If the junk dealer can't or won't test it, go somewhere else. Also, find out from which car in the junkyard the part came. If you're thinking of buying a used radiator that came from a car with front-end damage, chances are the radiator is damaged also.

The third reason you might want to sell your car is that the cost per mile to operate it has become too high. To make a decision whether to sell or keep your car based on cost per mile of operation, you must keep careful financial records. Use the example in Table 15-1 as a guide in calculating your cost per mile. In the example, we use the straight line depreciation method (10% per year) over 10 years for simplicity sake. Some cars depreciate more quickly in the early years than others. A big car may lose 25% of its value during the first year, 12% the second year, and less amounts thereafter. A small car would probably more closely fit our example of an average 10%-per-year depreciation.

16

Minor Maintenance Activities

THIS CHAPTER CONTAINS PROCEDURES AND INSTRUCTIONS THAT CAN BE USED TO PERFORM a number of maintenance activities for your car. These activities are by no means exhaustive. There are additional preventive maintenance activities referenced in preceeding chapters that should be performed at the recommended intervals. The preventive maintenance items chosen for this chapter are some of the more important ones we all need to perform to get long life from our cars.

OIL AND FILTER CHANGES

Frequency: Every 3000 miles

Tools and Supplies:

- —Trouble light
- —Oil drain wrench or crescent wrench
- —Oil filter cartridge wrench
- —Car ramps or stand jacks
- —Oil drain pan
- —Funnel
- —New oil filter
- —New oil (amount specified in owner or shop manual)
- —Some lint-free cloths or rags
- —Tarp or old blanket to lie on

Procedure:

1. Bring the engine to operating temperature so that any sludge at the bottom of the oil pan will drain freely.
2. Drive the car onto car ramps or jack it up and place it on stand jacks. Use caution in either case. Block the rear wheels and set the parking brake on (Figs. 16-1 and 16-2).
3. If the car has an automatic transmission place the shift in PARK. If the car has a manual transmission place the shift in REVERSE.
4. Remove the oil filler cap.
5. Position the oil drain pan underneath the drain plug in the bottom of the oil reservoir. Refer to the owner or shop manual to locate the plug (Fig. 16-3).
6. Loosen the oil drain plug with the oil drain wrench until it is just about ready to fall out. Then remove it quickly by hand, being careful not to burn yourself with hot oil. Try not to let the drain plug fall into the drain pan.
7. Let the oil drain until all the flow stops. Inspect the oil drain plug. Make sure the drain plug gasket (if equipped) is in good condition. Reinstall the drain plug and tighten firmly.
8. Move the drain pan underneath the location of the oil filter. Loosen the oil filter with the oil filter wrench, then finish removing by hand. Drain any oil inside the filter cartridge into the drain pan.
9. Before installing the new oil filter, clean the oil filter seat on the engine with a lint-free cloth. Wipe a light film of clean engine oil on the new filter rubber gasket and install the new filter. Tighten the new filter by hand per the shop manual instructions. Don't overtighten, you could distort the rubber gasket, causing it to leak.
10. Pour the specified amount of new oil into the engine at the oil filler hole, using a funnel to avoid spills.

Fig. 16-1. Vehicle properly mounted on ramps.

Fig. 16-2. Vehicle properly mounted in jack stands.

Fig. 16-3. Placing oil pan under car.

11. Reinstall the oil filler cap.
12. Run the engine for a few minutes, then turn the engine off and check for signs of oil leakage at the filter and drain plug. Also, check the dipstick for indication of proper oil level.
13. Remove the car from the ramps or stand jacks.
14. Dispose of the used oil properly. Empty it into old milk jugs or into empty oil cans or bottles. Some gas stations will accept used oil for recycling.
15. Record the date and mileage for the oil and filter change.
16. Check the oil level every day for a few days after the oil change to make sure no oil is being lost through leakage.

THE GREASE JOB

Combine this job with the oil/filter change if possible.

Frequency: Every 6000 miles.

Tools and Supplies:

—Trouble light
—Car ramps or stand jacks
—Tarp or old blanket to lie on
—Grease gun
—Grease gun cartridge
—Rags
—Shop manual drawing showing location of grease fittings

Procedure: (Note—Follow all established safety procedures for jacking a car.)

1. Drive the front of the car onto car ramps or jack it up and place it on stand jacks. Use caution in either case. Block the rear wheels and set the parking brake on. (See Figs. 16-1 and 16-2.)
2. If the car has an automatic transmission place the shift in PARK. If the car has a manual transmission place the shift in REVERSE.
3. Load the grease gun with a cartridge of grease of the proper type (Fig. 16-4).
4. Position the tarp or blanket underneath the front of the car. Locate and wipe clean all the grease fittings on the steering linkages and ball joints (Fig. 16-5).
5. Pump grease into each fitting until the boot at each location swells with grease. Note that some manufacturers install ball joints with plastic sleeves that do not require or allow greasing. Consult your shop manual to be sure. After the fitting has taken the required amount of grease, wipe it clean and go on to the next fitting.
6. Replace any fittings that do not take grease.
7. While the car is elevated, grease any transmission linkages that require periodic lubrication. Use the proper type of grease.
8. Remove the car from the ramps or stand jacks.

Fig. 16-4. Cartridge for grease gun.

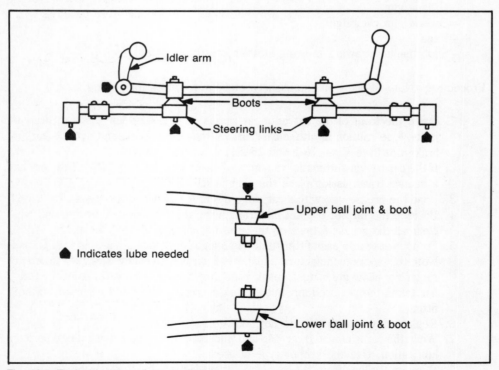

Fig. 16-5. Typical location of grease fittings.

9. Move to the rear of the car. Remove the fill plug on the differential case and check for the proper amount of lubricant. Fill as required and replace the plug.
10. Properly dispose of grease rags and empty grease cartridges.
11. Record the date and mileage for the grease job.

AUTOMATIC TRANSMISSION SERVICE

Frequency: Every 25,000 miles, or every 10,000 miles if towing.

Tools and Supplies:

—Trouble light
—Car ramps or stand jacks
—Oil drain pan
—Funnel
—New automatic transmission fluid (amount and type specified in owner or shop manual)
—Rebuild kit for cleaning pan
—Wrenches to fit pan cover
—Clean, lint-free cloths or rags
—Tarp or old blanket to lie on

Procedure: (Note—follow all established safety procedures for jacking a car.)

1. Drive the car onto car ramps or jack it up and place it on stand jacks. Use caution in either case. Block the rear wheels and set the parking brake on. (See Figs. 16-1 and 16-2.)
2. Place the shift in PARK.
3. Remove the transmission dipstick. Inspect the fluid on the stick for signs of trouble.
4. Place tarp or blanket under transmission.
5. Drain the transmission of all fluid into the oil drain pan. Refer to the instructions in the shop manual.
6. Remove transmission pan from bottom of transmission case (Fig. 16-6). Inspect the pan for sediment. Wipe clean with a lint-free cloth.

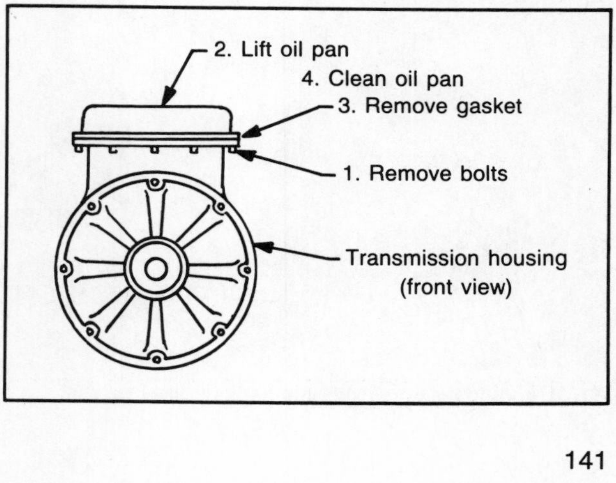

Fig. 16-6. Oil pan removal—clean dirt in bottom of pan.

2. Lift oil pan
4. Clean oil pan
3. Remove gasket
1. Remove bolts
Transmission housing (front view)

7. Inspect the transmission fluid screen for dirt (Fig. 16-7). Clean, if necessary, in appropriate solvent.

8. After everything is clean, reinstall the screen and pan with the new parts in the rebuild kit according to the kit instructions (Fig. 16-8). Bolt the pan to the transmission housing according to the instructions in the shop manual.

9. Refill the transmission with the proper amount and type of automatic transmission fluid. Do not overfill. Check for leaks around the pan. Reinstall the dipstick.

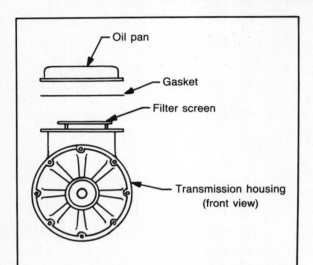

Fig. 16-7. Transmission filter screen.

Fig. 16-8. Automatic transmission pan and filter kit.

10. With the transmission at the factory recommended operating temperature, check the fluid level.
11. Remove the tarp or blanket.
12. Properly discard the old transmission fluid. Empty it into old milk jugs or into empty oil cans or bottles. Some gas stations will accept used transmission fluid for recycling.
13. Lower the car off the ramps or stand jacks.
14. Record the date and mileage for this service.

CHANGING V-BELTS

Frequency: When inspection indicates a change is needed, or monthly.

Tools and Supplies:

- —Fender cover
- —Set of box wrenches or sockets with driver
- —Crow bar or other pry bar
- —Belt tension gauge
- —New V-belt to suit application
- —Rags

Procedure:

1. Inspect the belt for fraying, tearing, or glossing. If the belt exhibits any of these conditions it should be replaced (Figs. 16-9 and 16-10).
2. Loosen the tension bracket for the belt. The tension bracket is normally the

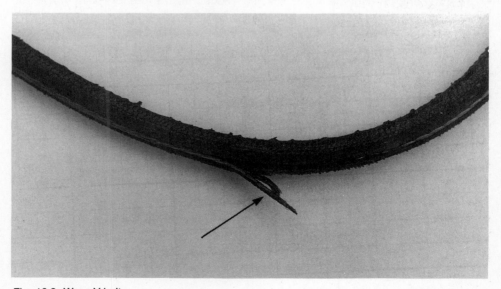

Fig. 16-9. Worn V-belt.

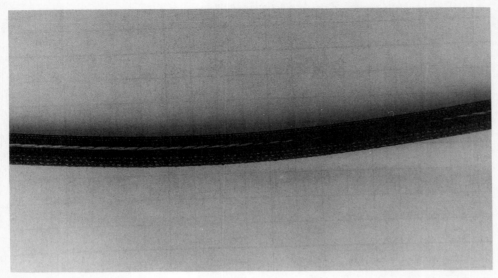

Fig. 16-10. New V-belt.

one holding the alternator in place. Consult the shop manual for the proper bracket or brackets for your car.

3. With the bracket loosened the old belt should slip off easily. If it doesn't readily come off the pulley, carefully use a pry bar to slip the belt. Be careful not to nick any of the pulley surfaces because nicks and scratches will quickly tear up the new belt.

4. Wipe the pulley with a clean, dry rag. Use cleaner if necessary.

5. Loop the new belt around the pulley, using the pry bar if necessary. Tighten the bracket until the belt flexes only about 1 inch. From this point on use the tension gauge to properly tension the belt. The shop manual will provide the proper settings of and location for the tensioner on the belt.

6. Run the engine at idle to check operation of the belt. It should not wobble or travel laterally on the pulley.

7. After a few days of operation on the road, check the belt tension again. Readjust if necessary.

8. Properly discard the worn V-belt.

9. Record the date and mileage the belt was changed.

CHANGING HOSES

Frequency: Every year or when inspection indicates a change is needed.

Tools and Supplies:

—Drain pan
—Antifreeze mix
—Funnel
—Spade type or flat screwdriver

—Tube of gasket sealer (only if required by shop manual)
—Replacement hose
—Replacement hose clamps (screw type)
—Utility knife
—Emery cloth
—Cloths or rags

Procedure: (Note—this procedure applies to changing heater and radiator hoses.)

Heater Hoses

1. Inspect the heater hoses for leaks, bubbling of the hose wall and fraying. If the hose exhibits any of these conditions or is very old, replace it (Fig. 16-11).
2. Unsnap or unscrew the hose clamps located at both ends of the hose. Remove the hose.
3. Stuff a cork or rag in or tape the openings of the fittings that the hose fits onto to prevent excessive antifreeze leakage when the hose is removed. Otherwise, drain the cooling system.
4. Inspect the fittings. Lightly sand any corrosion deposits or bits of hose or dirt from the fittings with the emery cloth. Clean and wipe dry.
5. Cut a length of replacement hose of the proper size and type the same length as the old hose. Remove any tape or other obstruction used to plug the fittings or refill the cooling system.
6. If your shop manual advises using gasket sealer or cement, apply it to the fittings only—not the inside of the hose ends.

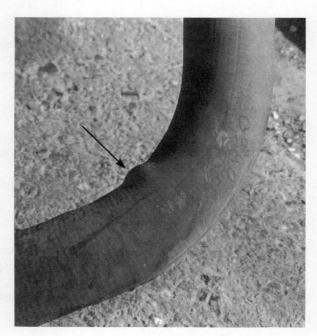

Fig. 16-11. Coolant hose with bubble.

Fig. 16-12. Spring-type hose clamp.

Fig. 16-13. Screw-type hose clamp.

7. Otherwise, slip hose clamps over the hose ends and then gently, but firmly, push the hose over the fittings the recommended amount. Twisting the hose slightly on the fitting as you push may help with getting the hose installed.
8. Replace the older design spring type hose clamps with screw type clamps (Figs. 16-12 and 16-13).
9. Tighten the hose clamps until firm, but not so tight that you begin cutting the hose with the clamp.
10. Refill the radiator or overflow tank making up for lost antifreeze.
11. Run the engine a few minutes checking for leaks.
12. Properly discard the old hoses.
13. Record the date and mileage of the hose replacement.

Radiator Hose

1. Inspect the radiator hoses for leaks and firmness of the hose wall. The hose should not feel soft or flimsy. If the hose is leaking or soft or is very old, replace it.
2. Drain the radiator, saving the fluid.
3. Unscrew the radiator hose clamps located at both ends of the radiator hose. Remove the old hose.

4. Inspect the fittings. Lightly sand any corrosion deposits or bits of hose or dirt from the fittings with the emery cloth. Clean and wipe dry.

5. If your shop manual advises using gasket sealer or cement, apply it to the fittings only—not the inside of the hose ends.

6. Otherwise, slip hose clamps over the hose ends and then push the hose over the fittings the recommended amount. If you encounter trouble getting the hose on the fittings, twist it back and forth slightly as you push until it is properly installed.

7. Tighten the hose clamps until firm, but not so tight that you begin cutting into the hose with the clamp.

8. Refill the radiator.

9. Run the engine a few minutes checking for leaks.

10. Properly discard the old radiator hose.

11. Record the date and mileage of the hose replacement.

CHANGING TIRES

Frequency: For rotation at 12,000 miles and to install snow tires.

Tools and Supplies:

—Proper jack for the car—see owner or shop manual
—Lug wrench
—Rags
—Penetrating oil
—Large flat screwdriver

Procedure:

1. Refer to the owner or shop manual for the proper position to place the jack. Follow the directions carefully. Avoid any shortcuts; safety first when using car jacks.

2. Before you raise the car remove the hub caps. Pry them off with the lug wrench or a large, flat screwdriver.

3. Jack up the corner of the car you want to work on first. If you are using a bumper jack make sure it's straight and firmly grounded so it can't tip over.

4. Before the wheel leaves the ground as you are jacking it upwards, loosen the lug nuts but don't remove them from the lugs just yet. Use penetrating oil if the nuts stick.

5. Continue raising the car just enough to gain the clearance between the tire and ground to remove the tire.

6. Remove the lug nuts, placing them inside the hub cap or some other secure place.

7. Slip the tire off the lugs.

8. Slip the replacement tire on the lugs, being careful not to scrape the lug threads.

9. Spin the lug nuts onto the lugs finger-tight.

10. Lower the car until the wheel just begins to make contact with the ground.

Tighten the lug nuts. Tighten one nut then proceed across the hub to another nut. Continue this crisscross pattern of tightening until all the nuts are tightened.

11. Finish lowering the car and install the hub cap.
12. Proceed to the next wheel.
13. Store tires that are to be saved properly.
14. Record the date and mileage of the tire change.

SERVICING SHOCKS AND MUFFLERS

Frequency: Replace shocks every 25,000 miles, mufflers when they leak or are rusted through.

Tools and Supplies:

—Socket wrench set
—Pry bars, slittler, tailpipe cutter, and pipe expander
—Hammer
—Large flat screwdriver
—Penetrating oil
—Rags
—Heavy gloves
—New shock absorbers and/or bushings
—New muffler and hangers
—Exhaust system sealer

Procedure:

Shock Absorbers

1. Raise the car and support it as instructed in the service manual. This is very important: With a shock absorber removed the suspension could slip out of place in some models.
2. Soak both upper and lower shock mount bolts with penetrating oil and wait about 15 minutes. This will make the job much easier.
3. Remove the shock from the mount with the proper size rachet wrench.
4. Inspect the shock for damage, leaks, and loss of resistance. Shocks cannot be repaired, so replace them—in pairs—if they exhibit any signs of trouble.
5. If the shock seems in good shape, inspect the rubber bushings. Perhaps the bushings are worn and are the real problem. Replace them and reinstall the shock. Otherwise, a new shock plus bushings are needed.
6. Tighten shocks only the recommended amount, as specified in the instructions that come with the shocks or as stated in the service manual.
7. Lower the car and road test.
8. Properly dispose of old shock absorbers.
9. Record the date and mileage of the shock absorber replacement.

Mufflers

1. Raise the car and support it as instructed in the service manual.
2. Inspect the muffler. Small holes caused by road debris may be repaired with a muffler repair kit available from auto stores.
3. Holes caused by rust-through or corrosion cannot normally be repaired very well and even if they can, the repair will not last long. It's better to replace the muffler.
4. Stuff a rag into the end of the tailpipe with the engine running. If you hear any hissing sound the muffler is leaking and needs replacement (Fig. 16-14).
5. Carefully remove the muffler. If you plan to save the exhaust pipe, extension pipe, or tailpipe, be extra careful disconnecting the muffler from them. Sometimes removing a muffler is a tough job, so proceed slowly and deliberately. Wear heavy gloves to protect your hands from sharp metal edges.
6. Use the slittler and hammer to gradually peel away pipe ends for ease of removal. Consult the service manual for detailed instructions on removal.
7. Replace any broken or damaged hangers after the muffler is off (Fig. 16-15).
8. To salvage pipes, use a pipe expander to remove pipe clamp grooves and restore the pipe to its original size. Follow the directions that come with the tool.
9. Install the new muffler, coating the connections with exhaust system sealer or muffler cement.
10. Lower the car and road test. Make sure the muffler doesn't wiggle or thump by road testing when the job is done.
11. Properly discard the used muffler.
12. Record the date and mileage of the muffler replacement.

Fig. 16-14. Rusted muffler.

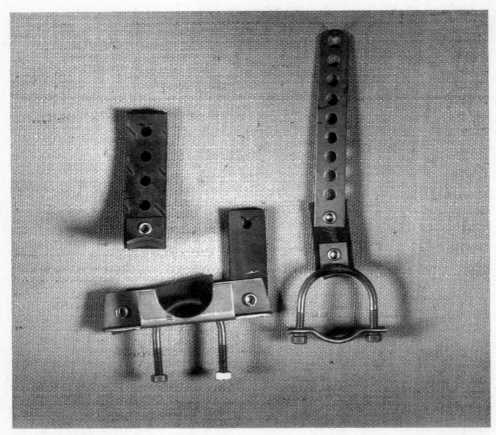

Fig. 16-15. Various pipe and muffler hangers.

DEGREASING THE ENGINE

Frequency: Twice a year or at tune-up time.

Tools and Supplies:

—Engine degreaser (Fig. 16-16)
—Aluminum foil or plastic wrap
—Rubber bands
—Duct tape
—Garden hose
—Old rags

Procedure:

1. Remove the air cleaner assembly. Cover the top of the carburetor with foil or plastic wrap and secure with a rubber band or duct tape (Fig. 16-17).

Fig. 16-16. Engine degreasers.

Fig. 16-17. Protecting the carburetor with aluminum foil.

2. Cover the distributor in the same manner.
3. Disconnect the battery cables and remove the battery. Cover the cable ends with foil or plastic.
4. Remove large chunks of grease with a rag. Wipe off excessive oil, also with a rag.
5. Follow the directions on the can of degreaser. Spray all areas to be cleaned with a thick foamy coating of degreaser. Wait the required amount of time.
6. Remove the foam and grease according to directions—usually this is done by spraying with a garden hose.
7. Finish by wiping difficult areas to remove residual grease. If necessary, reapply degreaser for a second treatment.
8. Uncover the carburetor, battery cables, and distributor. Reinstall the battery.
9. Record the date and mileage of the degreasing job.

SERVICING A CARBURETOR

Frequency: Twice a year.

Tools and Supplies:

—Tachometer
—Screwdrivers
—Socket wrench set
—Carburetor cleaner
—Pliers
—Thickness gauges
—Rags
—Carburetor adjustment specifications

Procedure:

1. Remove the air cleaner assembly.
2. Clean the entire exterior of the carburetor with carburetor cleaner.
3. Run the engine until it reaches operating temperature, then spray carburetor cleaner down the carburetor throat until all deposits are removed.
4. Adjust the idle speed to specification using the tachometer. Check the service manual for special instructions before proceeding.
5. While watching the tachometer gauge, turn the idle speed adjusting screw to bring the idle speed to specification. Turning the screw inward increases idle speed and outward decreases idle speed. See Fig. 16-18.
6. If the car has a throttle stop modulator, check it next. This modulator prevents continued running of the engine after the engine is turned off (dieseling). Locate the throttle stop modulator by referring to the service manual.
7. While an assistant shuts off the engine, check to make sure the modulator plunger retracts by closing the throttle. If there is a problem with the modulator you'll have to buy a new one; it can't be repaired.
8. Find the location of the idle mixture screws. With the engine running, turn the screws in slowly until the engine begins to run roughly. This means the mixture

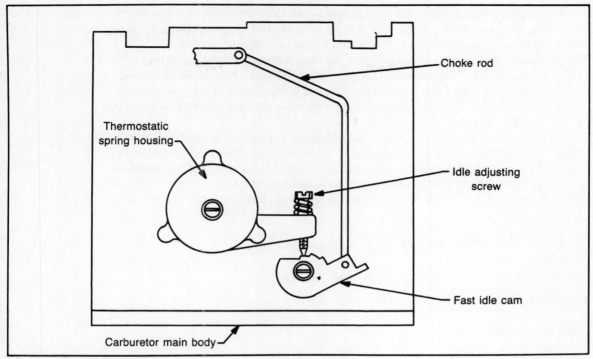

Fig. 16-18. Adjusting idle speed.

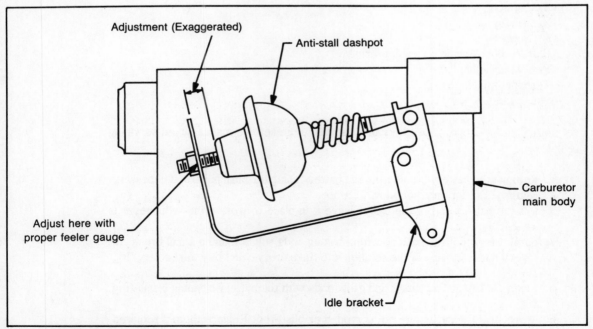

Fig. 16-19. Adjusting the dashpot.

of air and fuel is lean—not enough fuel. Turn the screws out until the engine runs rough from too rich a mix, then turn the screws in again halfway between the lean and rich settings to obtain the best idle mixture setting.

9. Locate the automatic choke. Spray carburetor cleaner on all the moving parts of the choke. Wipe clean and oil the parts lightly with mineral oil. Make sure all the choke linkages move freely. There are many types of automatic chokes. Check with the service manual for additional service and adjustments for your particular car.

10. Check and adjust the antistall dashpot if the carburetor is equipped with an externally mounted one. Refer to the service manual. Check the clearance between the dashpot and the carburetor lever with a feeler gauge. If an adjustment is needed, loosen the lock nut and turn the dashpot until the proper clearance—as measured by the thickness gauge—is obtained. Retighten the locknut (Fig. 16-19).

11. Install the air cleaner assembly.

12. Record the date and mileage of the carburetor service.

SERVICING THE BATTERY

Frequency: Twice a year. Clean case once a year.

Tools and Supplies:

- —Socket wrench set
- —Distilled water
- —Baking soda
- —Battery syringe
- —Hydrometer
- —Battery post/terminal cleaning brush
- —Petroleum jelly
- —Terminal puller
- —Small brush

Procedure: (Note—Follow the safety precautions in the service manual when servicing the battery.)

1. Remove the battery cables from the battery using terminal pullers, if necessary.

2. Remove the battery hold-down clamps.

3. Lift the battery out of the car or leave it in place to work on it—whichever is easiest for you.

4. Scrub the top of the battery with a baking soda solution and a small brush. Be careful not to get any of the solution into the battery cells. Dry the battery (Fig. 16-20).

5. Clean the battery terminals and cable ends with the battery cleaning brush (Fig. 16-21).

6. Make sure the cables are not corroded or blistered. Replace them if required.

Fig. 16-20. Dirt collects here on battery case.

Fig. 16-21. Cleaning the battery terminals.

Fig. 16-22. Checking the battery charge with hydrometer.

7. Install the cables onto the terminals. Coat them with petroleum jelly to avoid future corrosion.
8. Use the hydrometer to measure the specific gravity of the battery electrolyte. If the specific gravity of any cell is below 1.230, measured at 80 degrees Fahrenheit, the battery may have to be charged (Fig. 16-22).
9. Add any required distilled water to bring the electrolyte solution to the recommended full line with the battery syringe.
10. Refasten the battery hold-down clamps.
11. Record the date and mileage of the battery service.

(*Note:* The battery shown is a maintenance-free battery. If you remove the cell covers from this type of battery you may void the warranty. The covers must be resealed to avoid water loss. Therefore, perform this service only if you suspect a defective cell.)

CLEANING AND GAPPING THE SPARK PLUGS

Frequency: Twice a year or at every tune-up.

Tools and Supplies:

—Spark plug gauges and gap tool
—Ignition file
—Spark plug socket and wrench
—Rags
—Spark plugs

Fig. 16-23. Gapping the spark plug.

Fig. 16-24. Adjusting the electrode.

Procedure:

1. Remove the ignition cable from the spark plug, being careful not to pull the boot off the cable. Grab the boot, not the cable, when pulling.
2. Remove the plug with the proper size spark plug socket and wrench.
3. Inspect the plug for signs of engine trouble such as oil burning, oil fouling, and overheating of the plug. Take appropriate action.
4. Wipe or file deposits off the plug.
5. If the plug electrodes are worn too thin, replace the plug.
6. Gap the plug with the correct wire gauge using the gap tool to bend the side electrode (Figs. 16-23 and 16-24). Be careful not to bend the electrode too far or too many times; it could break off.
7. Install the spark plug into the engine. Be especially careful not to strip threads when installing the plugs.
8. Replace the ignition cable firmly over the spark plug.
9. Move on to the next plug and continue until all of them are done.
10. Properly discard any used plugs.
11. Record the date and mileage of the spark plug service.

SERVICING THE DISTRIBUTOR

Frequency: Twice a year or at every tune-up.

Tools and Supplies:

—Screwdriver
—Distributor cap
—Rotor
—Condenser (if equipped)
—Breaker points (if equipped)
—Ignition file
—Thickness gauges
—Needle-nose pliers
—Small wire brush
—Emery cloth (fine)

Procedure:

1. Remove the distributor cap and check for cracks. If cracked, replace it.
2. Remove the ignition wires from the distributor cap, being careful to note their correct terminal location. Mark them with tape and number them so you won't get them mixed up.
3. Using a small wire brush clean the inside of each cap terminal. Wipe the cap clean of all oil, grease, and road dirt that can cause voltage leaks.
4. Very lightly sand the inside contacts of the cap and the center rotor contact button to remove carbon. If you sand too heavily you will ruin the cap. Do not remove any metal from the contacts (Fig. 16-25).

Fig. 16-25. Wear occurs at terminal points of the distributor cap.

Fig. 16-26. Watch for wear of the rotor.

5. Attach the ignition cables to the distributor cap in the proper order and set the cap aside.
6. Remove the rotor and wipe·it clean with a dry cloth.
7. Inspect the rotor tip for chipping and burning. Scrape the tip clean if it's not too badly burned, but don't file it because that will increase the gap the spark must jump to the cap contacts. If in doubt, install a new rotor. Make sure the spring contact on top of the rotor has enough tension to make proper contact with the center contact button inside the cap (Fig. 16-26).
8. If the distributor has breaker points, remove them and inspect the contacts for pitting and burning. File lightly or replace them.
9. Install the breaker points and properly gap them with the thickness gauge. Refer to the service manual for specifications and correct installation instructions.
10. Install the rotor and cap.
11. Properly discard used parts.
12. Record the date and mileage of the distributor service.

REPAIRING MINOR RUST

Frequency: Before minor rust turns into major rust-through.

Tools and Supplies:

—Power drill
—Wire brush for drill
—Degreaser
—Sandpaper
—Masking tape
—Primer paint
—Touch-up paint
—Wax

Procedure:

1. Inspect the car body for minor rust. Minor rust can be defined as surface rust that is less than one quarter of the thickness of the metal.
2. Look for minor rust around body trim moldings and all along the lower part of the body, especially at door bottoms.
3. Remove the rust with the brush and power drill until you get down to bright metal.
4. Lightly sand the surrounding edges of the paint, feathering them flush to the bright metal.
5. Clean the area with a degreaser such as carbon tetrachloride or some other commercially available product.
6. As soon as possible, apply primer to the bare metal according to the instructions on the bottle or can and let dry. Mask the area if need be to keep primer off good paint.

7. When sufficiently dry, apply touch-up paint over the primer. If more than one coat is necessary, sand lightly between coats for better adhesion.
8. Wax the area for protection.

FLUSHING THE COOLING SYSTEM

Frequency: Every 12,000 miles.

Tools and Supplies:

—Chemical flush solution
—T-connection
—Antifreeze
—Garden hose

Procedure:

1. Drain the cooling system. Use old milk jugs to dispose of the antifreeze.
2. Install a T-connection kit for flushing (Fig. 16-27). It is installed permanently.
3. Follow the instructions provided with the chemical flush and the T-connection kit for flushing.
4. Remove the cap from the T-connection and attach the garden hose.
5. Remove the radiator cap. Install the plastic deflector from the T-connection kit and tighten it in the radiator filter neck.

Fig. 16-27. Cooling system T-connection for flushing.

6. Turn on the garden hose. Water will flow out the plastic deflector. Make sure all the antifreeze is flushed out.
7. Add the chemical flush solution according to the directions on the can or bottle and reflush.
8. After flushing and disconnecting the garden hose, refill the cooling system with fresh antifreeze of the proper mix.
9. Run the engine with the radiator cap off for a few minutes to circulate fluid through the cooling system. Keep adding antifreeze until the system is full.
10. Install the radiator cap and clean up any spilled antifreeze.
11. Make sure the T-connection is properly closed off to prevent coolant leakage.

A Short Course in Buying a Used Car

SHOPPING FOR A USED CAR IS A DIFFICULT PROJECT. YOU NEVER KNOW HOW THE PREVIOUS owner cared for it and drove it. The previous owner might have sold it in order to escape expensive repairs or maintenance.

Below is a collection of tips in checklist form that will help you in selecting a used car. There is no guarantee that by following the advice presented here you won't get a bum deal. However, you stand a much improved chance of buying a good used car at least knowing what problems you face. Try to eliminate surprises as much as possible.

First, when you spot a good looking car that appeals to you, find the value of the car. You can do this by checking the NADA Official Used Car Price Guide. Banks, libraries, and credit unions carry the latest addition. Find the value of the car in the NADA Guide, being sure to include the value of all accessories such as power steering, air conditioning, etc. Save this figure and compare it to the dealer asking price. If the dealer wants too much more than the NADA value and won't budge on price, forget the car (perhaps the dealer, too!) and move on to something else.

Check on the recall history of the car. Have the dealer supply you with the manufacturer's customer service telephone number. Call the customer service representatives and give them the vehicle identification number. They can tell you if the car was ever involved in a recall and if the previous owner complied with the recall by having the necessary repairs made. You can also obtain general recall information by calling the National Highway Traffic Safety Administration (NHTSA) at 800-424-9393.

Years ago, it was common practice for unscrupulous used car dealers to tamper with the odometer by turning it back thousands of miles. What you thought was a car with 25,000 miles on it may have had, in reality, 75,000 or more miles on it. This is illegal today. Also, car manufacturers have installed anti-tampering devices on modern cars to thwart turning the odometer. In Ford and AMC cars, the odometer will break if it's tampered with. In GM cars, an odometer that was turned back will exhibit white lines between the numbers. And, in Chrysler products, if the ten-thousandth digits are colored blue the odometer has either turned past 100,000 miles or has been tampered with.

What about warranties? Primarily, warranties are given on used cars to get you to buy—another sales gimmick. Most of them aren't worth the paper they are written on. Unlike new car full warranties, used car warranties are limited warranties. They cover certain items for a short period of time, usually 30 to 90 days or 1,000 miles. They are hard to collect on. Should you have a claim on a used car under limited warranty and the dealer won't honor it, the only remedy you have is through legal action. Legal action can be expensive and time consuming. Before suing, have your lawyer write a letter to the dealer reminding him of his obligations under the law. Have your lawyer quote the Uniform Commercial Code, effective in most states, or the Magnuson-Moss Warranty—Federal Trade Commission Improvement Act Public Law 93–673 January 4, 1975. If you can't frighten the dealer into honoring your claim, you need to decide what is cheaper: suing for repairs and paying the lawyer or swallowing your pride and making repairs yourself.

So where's the best place to look for a used car? New car dealers who maintain a used car lot are the best bet. The cars bought there will be more expensive, but chances are, they will be in better shape. Most of the established, new car dealers offer dependable warranties they honor for up to 90 days in some cases. Don't buy a used car from a rental company. Those cars are used by people who have little interest in how they drive them. And frequently, although not always, they are poorly maintained. If you buy a used car from a rental company, demand to see the service record before you purchase. Buying privately can be a nightmare also, unless you know the party selling. You may get a used car by buying privately at up to 30% lower price compared to a dealer buy. If something goes wrong, however, you have no legal recourse unless you can prove deliberate fraud.

Before you hit the streets looking for your dream car, consult one of the leading consumer publications for information on frequency of repair and owner satisfaction for the used car you're considering buying. Your best bet is a low-mileage (below 40,000), 4-door sedan with a medium size engine (six or small V-8). Also, consider buying one with an automatic transmission without air conditioning.

Feel free to take the checklist below with you on your hunt. Check the items in the order listed. Items that indicate major repairs top the list. If you record too many negatives right from the start it's better to seek another car. And one last point, take a friend along and shop during the day. Night lighting has a way of making the poorest paint sparkle. Your friend, who has no personal interest in the car, won't be dazzled by all the glitter and hard sell.

Used Car Buying Checklist
Category I - Items Indicating Major Repairs

ITEM	REF.	EVALUATION	PASS	FAIL
Engine Oil	Ch. 3	Check appearance, feel.		
		If drop of oil sizzles on hot engine, oil is fouled with coolant.		
		Engine should not be oil covered.		
		No oil in air cleaner.		
		Check plugs for oil fouling.		
		Oil pressure at idle about 15 psi.		
		Oil pressure at run 40 to 60 psi.		
Automatic Transmission Fluid and Transmission	Ch. 5	Check fluid appearance, feel, smell.		
		Transmission shifts smoothly.		
		Transmission should not be noisy.		
Radiator/ Coolant	Ch. 12	Check coolant appearance for signs of rust or oil.		
		Check radiator for leaks.		
		Check radiator cap.		
		Check coolant hoses.		
Engine Performance	Ch. 8/9	Engine should not buck or hesitate upon acceleration.		
		Engine should not exhaust black, white, blue- gray smoke.		
		Engine should not emit strange noises.		
		Engine should restart easily when hot.		
		Engine temperature should remain normal at all speeds/conditions.		
Body	Ch. 11	Check for rust.		
		Check for blisters in paint.		

ITEM	REF.	EVALUATION	PASS	FAIL
Body		Check quality of repaint job.		
		Compare width of crack around doors, hood, and trunk on both sides of car. Cracks wider on one side indicate damage to body.		
		Check for quality of repairs.		
		Check trunk for rust.		
Clutch	N/A	Run the engine at idle with parking brake on.		
		Shift into first. Rev engine at fast idle. Slowly release clutch. When clutch is ¾ of the way out, engine should stall. Otherwise new clutch is needed.		
Suspension/ Steering	Ch. 4/7	Wheels should not wobble.		
		Check suspension over bumpy roads.		
		Check shock absorbers.		
		Check wheels for looseness.		
		Steering should not be loose or sloppy.		
		Car should not pull to one side on level, straight road.		
Brakes	Ch. 7	Brakes should stop car smoothly.		
		Brakes should not squeal, fade, or grab.		
		Parking brake should hold the car on a hill.		
		Brake fluid should be within ½ inch of top of master cylinder.		
		Check for brake fluid leaks.		
		Brake pedal should not go to within 1 inch of floor when depressed.		
Misc. Accessories	Ch. 7/9/12	Check for bearing noise in water pump.		
		Check for bearing noise in alternator.		

ITEM	REF.	EVALUATION	PASS	FAIL
		Power steering system fluid level should be full.		
		Check exhaust system for leaks, holes, and patches.		
Belts/ Hoses	Ch. 6	Check all belts for condition.		
		Check all hoses for condition.		
Tires	Ch. 6	Check tires for wear. One-half or more tread left is passable.		
		Check tires for abnormal wear. If tires are retread—Fail.		
Battery	Ch. 9	Check battery case for cracks.		
		Check battery case and cables for corrosion.		
		Check charge of battery.		
Interior	Ch. 11/12	Check wear of upholstery— wear, tears, rips, burns, punctures, etc.		
		Check condition of floor mats.		
		Check wear of pedals.		
		Check for flooding—musty odor, water marks, corroded fuse panel.		
		Check under seat covers, if installed.		
		Operate windows, mirrors, doors.		
		Operate all accessories.		
Exterior	Ch. 11	Operate exterior lights.		
		Operate turn signals.		
		Operate trunk, hood, and locks.		
		Check trunk for jack and spare tire.		

Appendix B

Metal Fatigue

THE DICTIONARY DEFINES FATIQUE AS WEARINESS FROM LABOR OR USE. NO DOUBT WE ALL have felt tired or fatigued at the end of a tough day, sometimes close to our breaking point. We want to stop, to give up, to relax. Strangely enough, metals exhibit this same sort of behavior, some sooner than others.

All metals are susceptible to some degree to fatigue damage or failure. True fatigue failures occur over relatively long periods of service life at stress levels higher than those normally considered during the design process. If you bend the wire of a paper clip back and forth, no apparent damage is done the first time or two. However, after repeated bending, the ductility of the wire is fatigued or exhausted, and breakage occurs. This is an illustration of very short-life, or low-cycle, fatigue failure.

Metal fatigue has been studied for well over 100 years. In 1869 A. Wohler, chief locomotive engineer of the Royal Lower Silesian Railways, Germany, discovered such important facts as: it is the number of stress cycles rather than the elapsed time of use that is important, and that ferrous materials can withstand an infinite number of stress cycles, providing the stresses are all below certain limiting values.

Modern fatigue studies took off, so to speak, in the aircraft industry. Aircraft manufacturing companies make extensive use of aluminum alloys in aircraft construction. Aluminum is very susceptible to fatigue damage at even low stress levels. Before fatigue was properly accounted for in design, the aluminum used to fabricate the body parts of the aircraft would very often mysteriously crack, especially with age, in wing and tail section areas where vibration and flexing are most exhibited. When engineers learned to keep the stress levels low in these areas and learned to minimize vibration or to design controlled vibration into these aircraft body sections, fatigue failures began to decline dramatically.

What does all this have to do with the car you drive back and forth to work, you might ask? Most, if not all, of the parts of today's cars that might be susceptible to fatigue damage are made from medium- to high-strength alloy steels. These parts include the crankshaft, the connecting rods, the pistons, engine springs, and any other parts that exhibit back-and-forth or flexure motion or are repeatedly stressed and unstressed. As we stated before, as long as these parts are made of a ferrous material—steel in these cases—and stresses are held below a certain limiting value, fatigue failures should not occur. All well and good!

Now let's suppose that you don't take the advice given in Chapter 3 in regard to frequent oil changes. Let's further suppose that you allow the oil to remain in the engine for 10,000 miles or more. That oil is going to be filthy, clogged with combustion products, and by then, probably void of any useful additives. In short, the ability of the oil to properly lubricate any of the moving parts of the engine is in serious question. Friction throughout the engine will increase significantly with subsequent additional loading put on the cooling system to remove the friction heat. As friction increases it will require more engine power to rotate the crankshaft, move the connecting rods, slide the pistons, etc.

As the engine strains to keep all these parts moving, it must apply more and more force on the parts as friction increases. As more force is applied to the moving parts to keep them working, the stress levels in those parts will rise. These higher stress levels are repeated with engine speed at up to 5,000 times per minute. Because these higher stress levels can easily surpass the limiting design value for infinite (long) life, fatigue damage will gradually occur and engine life will decline.

This material is included as a final effort to convince you to change oil regularly. It is so important to engine life that it cannot be overstated.

Appendix C

Maintenance Schedule and Record

USE THE FOLLOWING MAINTENANCE SCHEDULE/RECORD TO KEEP YOUR CAR IN TOP SHAPE and ensure its longevity and performance. The asterisks on each chart show exactly when each service should be performed, determined either by miles accumulated or by weekly, monthly, or yearly intervals.

APPENDIX C - MAINTENANCE SCHEDULE AND RECORD

SERVICE	3,000	5,000	12,000	25,000	50,000	75,000	100,000	WEEK	2 WEEK	MONTH	2 MONTH	6 MONTH	YEAR	2 YEAR
INTERVAL														
Check Oil Level								*						
Check Tire Inflation								*						
Check Coolant Level								*						
Check Other Fluid Levels								*						
Wash Car								*						
Check A-T Fluid Level									*					
Inspect All Belts/Hoses										*				
Clean Radiator										*				
Clean Upholstery										*				
Inspect Air/Fuel Filters											*			
Wipe Down Engine											*			
Wax Car											*			
Change Engine Oil	*													
Change Engine Oil Filter	*													

Note: *—denotes proper service interval. Record actual mileage or date service is performed directly on chart for a permanent service record.

171

APPENDIX C - MAINTENANCE SCHEDULE AND RECORD

SERVICE \ INTERVAL	3,000	5,000	12,000	25,000	50,000	75,000	100,000	WEEK	2 WEEK	MONTH	2 MONTH	6 MONTH	YEAR	2 YEAR
Grease Wheel Bearings	*													
Grease Steering Linkages	*													
Check Manual Trans. Lube Level	*													
Check Rear Axle Lube Level	*													
Check Steering Gear Box Lube	*													
Check PCV System		*												
Lube Door, Hood, Trunk Hinges												*		
Lube Clutch Cable (if equipped)												*		
Check Brake Fluid												*		
Adjust Shoe Type Brakes												*		
Perform Complete Tune-Up												*		
Check Air Conditioning												*		
Check/Adjust Shift & Throttle Linkages													*	
Check/Adjust Vacuum Modulator													*	

Note: * —denotes proper service interval. Record actual mileage or date service is performed directly on chart for a permanent service record.

APPENDIX C - MAINTENANCE SCHEDULE AND RECORD

INTERVAL / SERVICE	3,000	5,000	12,000	25,000	50,000	75,000	100,000	WEEK	2 WEEK	MONTH	2 MONTH	6 MONTH	YEAR	2 YEAR
Rotate Tires			*										*	
Inspect Misc. Rubber Parts													*	
Inspect Entire Brake System													*	
Use Cylinder Cleaner													*	
Test Fuel Pump			*										*	
Clean Battery Case													*	
Clean Battery Tray													*	
Check Radiator Cap													*	
Shampoo Carpets													*	
Adjust Valve Clearance			*											
Clean PCV System			*											
Flush Cooling System			*											
Clean Engine Oil Pan				*										*
Clean Engine Oil Pump Screen				*										*

Note: * —denotes proper service interval. Record actual mileage or date service is performed directly on chart for a permanent service record.

173

APPENDIX C - MAINTENANCE SCHEDULE AND RECORD

INTERVAL / SERVICE	3,000	5,000	12,000	25,000	50,000	75,000	100,000	WEEK	2 WEEK	MONTH	2 MONTH	6 MONTH	YEAR	2 YEAR
Change A-T Fluid				*										
Change A-T Pan/Filter				*										
Adjust A-T Bands				*										
Replace Shock Absorbers				*										
Replace Vacuum Hoses														*
Replace Distributor Cap/Rotor					*									
Test Alternator					*									
Test Starter						*								
Dress Valves							*							
Replace Alternator Brushes							*							
Replace Radiator Cap							*							

Note: *—denotes proper service interval. Record actual mileage or date service is performed directly on chart for a permanent service record.

174

Index

Index

177

Edited by Cherie R. Blazer / Joanne M. Slike

Other Bestsellers From TAB

☐ **DIESEL ENGINE MECHANICS—Wayne A. Kelm**

Packed with line drawings and illustrated diagrams, *Diesel Engine Mechanics* covers the construction, operation, and service of diesel engines commonly found in today's automotive, light construction, agricultural, industrial and marine type vehicles and equipment up to 100 hp. This guide can save hundreds of dollars by showing how you can maintain, troubleshoot, and repair these engines yourself. It also provides the sound, general foundation that is needed to begin a career in diesel mechanics. 288 pp., 265 illus.

Paper $16.95   **Hard $21.95**
Book No. 2780

☐ **THE METALWORKER'S BENCHTOP REFERENCE MANUAL—Joseph W. Serafin**

This one-stop, ready reference contains all the information and instructions on metalworking that you need to complete any metalworking endeavor. By illustrating new approaches and unusual machining methods it will help you solve practically any metalworking problem you encounter. The ideal answer book for anyone interested in the craft of metalworking, as well as for those in the profession, this all-encompassing sourcebook covers techniques for working with all types of metals. Packed with illustrations to ensure absolute understanding! 320 pp., 360 illus.

Paper $19.95   **Hard $25.95**
Book No. 2605

☐ **INSTALLING SUNROOFS AND T-TOPS—Carl Caiati**

Here's the complete illustrated guide to customizing almost any vehicle with a sunroof or T-top! Written by an automotive customizing expert, it covers everything from factory-installed units to luxury after-market conversions to do-it-yourself techniques. Packed with practical advice and professional tips, it includes a complete listing of sunroof and T-top models and manufacturers for dual and electric sunroofs! 176 pp., 154 illus.

Paper $12.95   **Hard $14.95**
Book No. 2132

☐ **CAR DESIGN: STRUCTURE & ARCHITECTURE—Jan P. Norbye**

Here's an inside look at automotive design—from the drawing board to the showroom floor . . . from the horseless carriage to the compact cars of the '80s! This book examines the reasons behind the positioning of the seats, engines, and other necessary elements, and how these choices affect the styling freedom of the body designer. 384 pp., 315 illus.

Paper $15.95   **Hard $20.50**
Book No. 2104

☐ **HOW TO CAST SMALL METAL AND RUBBER PARTS—2nd Edition—William A. Cannon**

Using this excellent sourcebook, you can easily make defect-free castings and at an amazingly low cost . . . obsolete or vintage car parts, hood ornaments, garden tools, kitchen utensils, automotive parts, replace antique parts, reproduce sculpture, and other art! Includes all-new information on casting polyurethane rubber parts. There's even a listing of sources for supplies and equipment. 176 pp., 143 illus.

Paper $12.95   **Hard $15.95**
Book No. 2614

☐ **CUSTOMIZING YOUR VAN—3rd Edition—Allan Girdler and Carl Caiati**

Panel, carpet, and personalize the interior of your van—add portholes, skylights, roof vents, fender flares—without spending a fortune at a professional conversion shop. You can give any van a new look that rivals the most elaborate of the "California Customs," and save money by doing it yourself! All the information—the techniques, the materials, and the step-by-step guidance—is here! 320 pp., 258 illus.

Paper $14.95   **Hard $18.95**
Book No. 2142

☐ **UNDERSTANDING AUTOMOTIVE SPECIFICATIONS AND DATA—James Flammang**

Do you feel like you have to be a mathematician to figure out all the numbers involved in automotive repair? Then you need this invaluable guide that explains all the numerical concepts you need to do tune-ups, overhauls, or adjustments, plus details on engine size, power, and economy. Amateur mechanics, and automobile enthusiasts will find this guide indispensable. 208 pp., 123 illus.

Paper $11.95   **Hard $12.95**
Book No. 2116

☐ **101 THINGS TO DO WITH YOUR CAR—Editors of *School Shop* Magazine**

A treasury of practical do-it-yourself projects to enhance the performance and prolong the life of your car! This is a "tool" that belongs on every car owner's workbench. You'll find a wealth of information to make you more knowledgeable about your car's modern transmission, fuel, electrical, exhaust, and other systems—know-how that may save you money when you need to take your car to a garage for more major repairs. 160 pp., 54 illus.

Paper $11.95   **Hard $15.95**
Book No. 2073

Other Bestsellers From TAB